T0267677

PUBLISHER'S NOTE

This paperback edition of *You'll Do: A History of Marrying for Reasons Other Than Love* has been published without the 73-page Notes section that appeared at the back of the original hardcover edition. Those endnotes, which feature sourcing citations as well as additional information and commentary, are available online at **youlldo.steerforth.com**.

YOU'LL DO

*A History of
Marrying for Reasons
Other Than Love*

MARCIA A. ZUG

STEERFORTH PRESS
LEBANON, NEW HAMPSHIRE

Image Credits:

Page 24: University of Michigan. The Weld-Grimke Manuscript Collection.

Page 68: Venereal Disease Visual History Archive. Courtesy of Erin Wuebker.

Page 71: The National Portrait Gallery, London, England. Licensed under CC BY-NC 4.0.

Page 117 (top): The New York Public Library.

Page 137: Smithsonian American Art Museum, The Ray Austrian Collection, gift of Beatrice L. Austrian, Caryl A. Austrian, and James A. Austrian.

For information about permission to reproduce selections from this book, write to:
Steerforth Press, 31 Hanover Street, Suite 1
Lebanon, New Hampshire 03766

Cataloging-in-Publication Data is available from the Library of Congress

ISBN 978-1-58642-396-4 (paperback)

Printed in the United States of America

Contents

To my parents, Joan and Chuck,
who married for love;

To my daughters, Willa and Lucy,
who I hope will marry for love;

And to my husband, Geordie,
who is sure to get grief for this book.

Introduction

First comes love. Then comes marriage.
Then comes the baby in the baby carriage.

— AMERICAN SCHOOLYARD RHYME

If you ask Americans why they married, almost everyone will say "love." Love is the only publicly acceptable reason to marry, but it is far from the only one. Despite romantic notions about love and marriage, marriage is fundamentally a legal institution. It is a way to confer valuable rights and benefits, and sometimes it is the only way to receive these rewards. A vast misconception about modern marriage is, as the nursery rhyme implies, love comes first. This isn't always true. Sometimes love comes later. Sometimes it doesn't come at all, and legally, love is irrelevant.

You'll Do was inspired by the marriage of my great-aunt Rosie, a brave woman who didn't marry for love. In the late 1930s, Rosie was working in a garment factory on Manhattan's Lower East Side. Like most of the workers, Rosie was Jewish. Her best friend in the factory was also Jewish, and both understood the dangers posed by the rise of fascism in Europe. Rosie and her friend were safe, but her friend's brother, Sol, was not. Sol lived in Poland and, as the Nazis rose to power, Sol's family began to fear for his life. They desperately sought to bring him to America, but the US's draconian immigration restrictions severely limited the immigration of "undesirable" groups, such as Jews. Sol was stuck. America would never grant his immigration application, with one exception — marriage. The only way to get Sol out of

Poland, and save his life, was to marry him. So that's what Rosie did. In late 1937, as Nazi Germany was preparing for war, Rosie left the safety of America to marry a man she had never met and save his life.

Sol entered the United States in September 1938. He moved in with Rosie; they had a daughter and fell in love. Rosie and Sol's story has a happy ending, yet it's a tale that haunts me. If Rosie hadn't married Sol, he almost certainly would have died in a Nazi concentration camp. Marriage saved his life, but only because a racist US immigration law denied him entry in the first place. *You'll Do* is full of similar stories. Stories that show how generations of American men and women have used marriage as a loophole to circumvent unfair or discriminatory laws. Unfortunately, not all these marriage stories are as admirable as Rosie's. *You'll Do* reveals how the rights and benefits that attach to marriage can also perpetuate harms. My family has a second, darker marriage story that falls into this category.

Many years ago, one of my relatives lived with his wife and daughter. The daughter was mentally disabled (it may have been a birth injury), and after her birth, the couple was unable to have more children. This caused them great sorrow, and when their daughter was grown, they paid a man to marry her and provide them with a grandchild. The marriage took place nearly a century ago, and the daughter's capacity to consent does not appear to have been an issue. The two were legally married, and shortly thereafter, the daughter fell pregnant. Then, having fulfilled the terms of the bargain, the husband disappeared. Nine months later, the daughter gave birth to a healthy baby.

This second story is about marrying for money, but it is also about marrying for parenthood and for criminal and legal protections. Marriage provided the husband with money while also protecting him from criminal prosecution for rape; there really isn't any other way to describe it. In addition, marriage gave the grandparents their longed-for second child and protected the child from the legal "taint" of bastardy.

The specifics of my family's stories are unique. However, their instrumental use of marriage is not. I have a neighbor who married to lower his university tuition, two friends who married for tax breaks, and a colleague who married for a green card. These four are just the ones who have told me about their non-love reasons for marrying. Presumably, I know many others. Chances are, you do as well. Perhaps a non-love reason even motivated your own marriage.

Historically, marrying for love was considered a gamble. A popular story from a 1791 issue of the *Virginia Gazette and Alexandria Advertiser* illustrates this pessimistic view. The story describes a beleaguered clergyman who was enduring a "curtain-lecture" (meaning a scolding) from his wife when they were interrupted by a young couple requesting a marriage ceremony. According to the article, "The poor Priest, actuated at that moment to his own feelings and particular experience," mistakenly began "repeating the burial Service." The "astonished Bridegroom" then pointed out the error, to which the clergyman replied, "I am obliged to marry you — but, believe me, my friend, you had better be buried." Between 1791 and 1823, this "anecdote" was printed more than sixty times.

Marrying for love was risky, and for centuries, many Americans believed marrying for the legal, social, and economic benefits attached to marriage was a safer bet. Blatantly transactional marriages were permissible and even admired. In 1821, the *Louisiana Gazette* printed a story of a young man who hedged his marital bets by auctioning himself off in a lottery. Described as "of a good figure and disposition," the man offered six hundred tickets for $50 each to single women interested in marriage. The winner was then "entitled to himself and the 30,000 dollars." The paper described the scheme as "ingenious" and expressed confidence that "matches formed this way" would "prov[e] as happy as those made in the usual manner."

Eventually, acceptance of transactional marriage had largely disappeared. By the late nineteenth century, the non-love match was viewed as threatening. The 1888 Supreme Court case *Maynard v. Hill* exemplified this change. In *Maynard*, the court described marriage as "an institution, in the maintenance of which in its purity the public is deeply interested, for it is the foundation of the family and of society, without which there could be neither civilization nor progress." Today, a century and a half later, such sentiments remain widespread. However, whether the *Maynard* court's fears were justified is a more complicated question.

Economists have long claimed that everything is already commodified, that such commodification is good, and that attempts to prevent the sale of certain goods and services are bad. Conversely, anti-commodificationists argue that viewing everything in market terms is detrimental and that such treatment coarsens and corrupts our world. Both views are likely correct. Feminist scholar Margaret Radin has dubbed this the double-bind problem and suggests that the best way to counteract it is to identify the underlying causes.

You'll Do examines the marriage double bind. It shows how the instrumental use of marriage can be beneficial, helping to combat racial, gender, and class discrimination, and how this calculated use of marriage can also further such oppression. Additionally, the book challenges the assumption that non-love marriages are problematic because love is the purpose of marriage. Since America's founding, marriage has primarily been a rights distribution mechanism. This remains the principal purpose of marriage, but that doesn't mean it should be. Marriage is an imprecise and unfair method for determining the allocation of rights and benefits. Decoupling these rewards from marriage would alleviate this unfairness. It would also, truly, make love the purpose of marriage. It might also make marriage obsolete.

You'll Do is divided into six chapters. Chapter 1 focuses on the best-known marital bargain — marrying for money. It traces the long history of "gold-digging" marriages and shows that marrying for money, especially by women, was expected and encouraged. Chapter 2 examines marrying for government benefits and highlights the government's extensive role in encouraging instrumental marriages. Chapter 3 explores the connection between marriage and status. It shows that married Americans have historically occupied a higher and more powerful status than the unmarried and that this connection continues to motivate modern marital decisions. Chapter 4 details the long-standing, but less well-known, criminal benefits that attach to marriage. Chapter 5 discusses the connection between marriage and parental rights, and chapter 6 returns to the issue of marrying for money, but with a focus on the present day.

You'll Do covers the most common non-love reasons people marry, with one significant exception — religion. In many religions, marriage is both a sacrament and a commandment. This can be a powerful non-love motivation for marriage. However, I have excluded religious marriage from *You'll Do* because the book's focus is on the connection between law and marital decision making. Religious marriages, if they comply with state marriage laws, receive the same legal benefits as all other marriages, but they are not motivated by these benefits. Spouses in religious unions would marry regardless of governmental recognition. Mormon polygamous marriages are one well-known example.

You'll Do is about the non-love reasons people marry, but even in these unions, love may be present. Marriage is complex, and people can marry for a combination of reasons. A person might decide to marry for immigration benefits, but only after also falling in love with their potential spouse; conversely, they might have loved their partner for many years, but only married when they decided to have a child. The purpose of this book is not to deny this complexity. Rather, *You'll Do* seeks to explore the consequences of a marital regime that insists love is the only acceptable reason to marry while enacting laws and policies that give Americans so many non-love reasons to wed.

chapter one

The Marital Bargain

*We state and affirm unambiguously, love
cannot extend its sway over a married couple.*

— QUEEN MARIE DE CHAMPAGNE

In 1812, Charlotte Lucas was no longer young. She was also plain and relatively poor. She had no job prospects and was a financial burden to her family. So, when a dull and dislikable but relatively well-off suitor proposed, she said yes. It was not a love match. Charlotte candidly described him as "neither sensible nor agreeable." Still, he had a good job and a steady income, and Charlotte considered it a fair trade. She would provide wifely services, homemaking and child-rearing, in exchange for financial security. Charlotte was content with her decision, but her friend Lizzie was appalled. Lizzie believed Charlotte was degrading herself; she couldn't imagine marrying for any reason other than love.

Charlotte and Lizzie are characters from Jane Austen's famous novel *Pride and Prejudice*. The novel idealizes romantic love yet also depicts the realities of its era. When Austen wrote *Pride and Prejudice*, marrying for love was desirable but not expected. The novel's opening line is explicitly about marrying for money: "It is a truth universally acknowledged that a gentleman in possession of a large fortune must be in search of a wife." While this sentence was intended to be humorous, it was also true. Nineteenth-century women were looking for

Jane Austen.

wealthy husbands. As historian Amanda Vickery writes, in
Georgian England "the length of a man's rent-roll remained the
ultimate aphrodisiac." Austen recognized this reality, even as she
lamented it. In a famous letter to her niece regarding marriage,
Austen wrote that there is "nothing worse than marrying without affection." She also noted, "Single women have a dreadful
propensity for being poor."

In early America, marriage was women's primary and
preferred financial option. In an exchange known as the marital bargain, women traded domestic services for economic
support. This practice of marrying for money was accepted
both because women lacked other financial options and because
such marriages posed no threat to male wealth. Under the law

of coverture, a seventeenth-century English doctrine governing marriage and adopted by the American colonies, a husband and wife were treated as a single person — the husband. Once married, wives had no legal claim to their husbands' money. They could not, practically speaking, marry for money. The most a woman could hope for when marrying a rich man was that he'd be willing to share. In contrast, men could absolutely marry for money. Upon marriage, husbands received immediate and total control over their wives' wealth. Consequently, despite their ability to pursue other economic opportunities, colonial men had a strong incentive to marry wealthy women.

Male Gold Diggers

Early American men's interest in marrying for money is apparent in various anti-gold-digging laws passed to thwart male fortune hunters. Age-of-consent restrictions were one of the clearest examples. These laws were intended to prevent mercenary males from targeting younger women based on the, likely correct, belief that teenage girls were particularly vulnerable to the charms of fortune hunters. In 1632, the Virginia Colony enacted the first age-of-consent law and prohibited children under the age of twenty-one from marrying without parental consent. The original law was gender-neutral, but when the law was amended in 1670, the legislature explained that its specific purpose was to prevent a child from being "ruynated in *her* fortunes." In 1696, the law was further revised to include monetary fines and jail time. It also included a provision decreeing that "any girl between the ages of twelve and sixteen who married without parental or guardian permission forfeited her inheritance to her next of kin." Similar provisions were adopted in North and South Carolina.

Colonial incest laws, and specifically the permissibility of cousin marriages, were also prompted by a desire to deter male fortune hunters. American women had the right to inherit but relinquished control over their inheritance upon marriage. As a result, a woman's inheritance could be lost to a gold-digging husband. Cousin marriage addressed this problem by increasing women's intrafamily marriage prospects and ensuring that family wealth remained in the family. Anti-gold-digging measures like age-of-consent and incest laws sought to deter fortune hunters, but their effectiveness was limited by the failure of state legislatures to acknowledge that the biggest incentive for male fortune hunting was married women's inability to own or control property. Eventually, married women's property acts were proposed to address these gold-digging incentives and provide a more effective solution.

In 1839, Mississippi passed the first married women's property act. According to the act's supporters, the purpose of the law was to protect women from mercenary or profligate husbands. As a Vicksburg, Mississippi, newspaper editorial explained, "The property of ladies should be guarded against the squandering habits of a drunken and gambling husband. The ladies are virtuous and prudent creatures — they never gamble, they never drink, and there is no good reason why the strong arm of legislation should not be extended to the protection of the property they bring into the marriage bargain." Similar sentiments were put forth by Mississippi state senator T. B. J. Hadley, the sponsor of the Mississippi married women's property act. Hadley wrote:

> [S]hall we, in this proud Republic, refuse to secure to [women] the certain possession of property to which they have as just a claim? Is there a wish of such gross injustice in the mind of any man that he would behold from woman the shield of protec-

tion which this bill proposes? Does man delight in woman's happiness? Then give them the plighted faith of our legislation, that they shall possess and enjoy the means of their own pleasure. I would sir, secure to them the product of their own labor — I would secure to them the possession of the property given them by fond parents or relatives. Secure this, sir — tis all I ask.

After the Mississippi act passed, other states began considering similar acts. They sought to give wives control over their money and protect them from mercenary or financially improvident husbands. In 1843, the *Tennessee Observer* argued in favor of a Tennessee married women's property act, noting, "The last few years have shown so much devastation of married women's property by the misfortunes of their husbands, that some new modification of the law seems the dictate of justice as well as prudence." That same year, the *Georgia Journal* expressed support for a Georgia act, writing that there was no good reason "why property bequeathed to a daughter should go to pay debts of which she knew nothing, had no agency in creating, and the payment of which, with her means, would reduce her and her children to beggary. This has been done in hundreds of instances, and should no longer be tolerated by the laws of the land."

One of the clearest discussions of these acts as an anti-gold-digging measure occurred during the 1868 South Carolina Constitutional Convention when the delegates were considering whether to include married women's property rights as part of the state's proposed constitution. South Carolina lawmaker J. H. Allen argued in favor of the provision, stating:

I appeal to you who have lived here all your lives, and seen women suffering from the hands of fortune

hunters; the plausible villains who, after securing
the property of their wives, have squandered it in
gambling and drinking, a class of men who are still
going about the country boasting that they intend
to marry a plantation, and take the woman as an
incumbrance.

Fellow lawmaker Benjamin Randolph, made similar arguments in support of the provision. He noted, "It is a common
thing for men to talk about marrying rich wives, and to marry
them for no other purpose than to squander their property."
These pleas were successful, and the South Carolina Constitution
was enacted with a provision guaranteeing married women the
right to own and convey property separate from their husbands'
property.

Married women's property acts drastically reduced the incentives for male gold digging. Men could still marry wealthy
women, and potentially share their fortune, but marriage
no longer guaranteed husbands a legal right to their wives'
wealth. In fact, once women controlled their money, it could be
extremely difficult for husbands to convince them to part with
it. The famous gold-digging marriage of Harriet Douglas and
Henry Cruger provided one such cautionary tale.

In the early nineteenth century, Harriet Douglas was a
wealthy New York heiress known for her red hair, her fiery
temper, and her love of European high society. Author Sir Water
Scott nicknamed Douglas the "lion-huntress of the social jungle"
because of her obsession with Europe's rich and famous. For
years Douglas traveled around the world, enjoying her freedom
and swearing she would never marry. Then, in 1833, at the age of
forty-three, she changed her mind and accepted the proposal of
her most dogged suitor, Henry Cruger, a handsome southern
lawyer ten years her junior.

A nineteenth-century political cartoon on conditions under coverture.

Cruger had worked hard for this marriage. For more than a decade, he had followed Douglas across the globe, plying her with love letters and making repeated and ardent declarations of devotion. When she finally accepted his proposal, Cruger believed his hard work had finally paid off; he would soon be a rich man. Then, Douglas presented her conditions. She would not relinquish her name (in fact she insisted he take her name), she would choose where they lived (upstate New York, which Cruger hated), and, most important, she would not cede control of her fortune. To ensure this last condition, Douglas instructed her lawyers to draft legal documents circumventing the traditional rules of coverture and ensuring she retained control of her money after marriage. Initially, Cruger refused to sign the papers, but he relented when he recognized Douglas was adamant. Cruger wanted Douglas's money, but he was confident he'd be able to change her mind after marriage. He was correct, but the battle was long and painful.

At first, Cruger played the doting husband. He naively believed that by agreeing to Douglas's requests and signing the property documents, Douglas would be so grateful that she would immediately relinquish her fortune. She did not. When that plan failed, Cruger's next strategy was to sow discord between Douglas and her brothers. He hoped this would increase her loyalty to him, but she chose her brothers. Then, after these first attempts were unsuccessful, Cruger tried pouting and complaining about his financial dependency. During one such tantrum, Cruger refused to drink wine, saying he did "not own it," and refused to go riding because he did "not own any carriage." When Douglas was unaffected by these antics, Cruger moved out, swearing he would not return until Douglas turned over her fortune; he caved when she refused.

Cruger's next idea was to use Douglas's friends against her, and this tactic was partially successful. After significant pressure from her friends, Douglas agreed to give Cruger a substantial yearly allowance, yet Cruger still wasn't satisfied. He continued to harass Douglas for her money and eventually, when she couldn't stand it anymore, she left him. Cruger was elated. This was the development he had been waiting for. He immediately embraced the role of the wronged husband and began writing letters to Douglas's family and church expressing his hurt and outrage at her disobedience and refusal to live with him. Eventually, the enormous disapproval of her friends, family, and church led Douglas to relinquish more than half her income to Cruger. After eight long years, Cruger had won — sort of. Shortly after agreeing to Cruger's demands, Douglas changed her mind. Another eight years passed before a court ruled her promise to share her fortune was enforceable.

HENDERSON HOUSE   JORDANVILLE, N.Y.

The mansion in upstate New York where Harriet Douglas and Henry Cruger lived, and which Cruger hated.

After Cruger's legal victory, the editor of the *New York Legal Observer* congratulated him for having "passed through this fiery ordeal unscathed, vindicated and triumphant." However, whether Cruger had emerged unharmed is debatable. It had taken him sixteen years to get Douglas's money (not including the decade he spent courting her), and along the way, his reputation had been ruined. Years later, composer George Templeton Strong unflatteringly described Cruger as a man who "lived for . . . twenty years on [money] extorted by process of law from a wife he hated and whom he had married for her money."

Cruger's good friend, author James Fenimore Cooper — the two had met during a European tour and became lifelong friends — was so disturbed by the difficulties Cruger endured that he wrote an entire novel depicting the horrors of the Douglas-Cruger marriage. The novel, *The Ways of the Hour*, was published two years after New York enacted its married women's property act and was intended as a warning about the "dangers" of female financial control. Cruger's difficulties were then further compounded by the fact that Douglas spent the rest of her life trashing Cruger's reputation. She is reported to have seated her frequent visitors on sofas made from the hacked-apart halves of her former marital bed while serenading them with the song "For love of gold he has left me."

Female Gold Diggers

By giving wives control over their fortunes, married women's property acts largely eliminated the legal incentives for male gold digging (few men wanted to be the next Henry Cruger), but these laws had little effect on whether women married for money. The average American woman didn't have a large inheritance or her own income; thus, marriage remained her primary means of securing financial support. In 1854, a satirical English pamphlet titled "Legal Condition of Unmarried Women or Spinster" highlighted women's lack of financial opportunities, noting that "Queen" was pretty much the only desirable job available to women. American women didn't even have that option.

In the nineteenth century, most female employment was low-paid misery, even for women in the middle class. For these women, governess was one of the only jobs available, and contemporary descriptions portray it as hellish. Author Mary Wollstonecraft likened becoming a governess to "going into the Bastille," and Jane Austen's description is even grimmer. Austen wrote that to become a governess means to "retire from all the pleasures of life, of rational intercourse, equal society, peace and hope, to penance and mortification forever." It is little wonder that women routinely married to avoid this fate. Charlotte Brontë's novel *Shirley* includes such a marriage. In *Shirley*, Mrs.

The Governess, Emily Mary Osborn, 1828–1925.

Pryor, a woman who abandoned her daughter as a small child, admits she "ought never to have married," but explains she did so because she "had been so miserable as a governess."

Nineteenth-century women lacked viable economic alternatives to marriage. Consequently, many agreed to exchange domestic services for financial support. This marital bargain was not a "sale," but there were uncomfortable similarities. Until the mid-nineteenth century, England even permitted couples to end their relationships through a type of informal divorce known as wife selling. This practice allowed a married couple to publicly sever financial ties to each other and begin a new relationship, but it also treated the wife, at least symbolically, as a commodity. To effect the "sale," a husband would place a halter around his wife's neck and bring her to the cattle market on market day.

A "wife sale."

He would then offer her to the "highest bidder" — the man she would have married had legal divorce been possible.

"Wife sales" were performances, yet the marital bargain unquestionably encouraged men, and the courts, to view wives in economic terms. Such treatment is apparent in judicial decisions like the 1886 Pennsylvania case *Gring v. Lerch*. In 1882, Charles Gring proposed to Clara Lerch and she accepted, but shortly thereafter, she informed Gring that she had an unusually "thickened hymen" and would need surgery before she could engage in intercourse. Lerch promised to schedule the surgery, but three months later, she still hadn't remedied her "physical defect." Gring broke off the engagement, and Lerch sued him for breach of promise to marry. Gring's defense was that Lerch's failure to remedy her "physical defect" meant she was unable to fulfill the "sexual duties of a wife"; therefore, he was "legally justified in ending the engagement."

In ruling for Gring, the court characterized marriage as an economic exchange in which a husband trades financial support for sexual intimacy. Lerch could not provide sex, hence Gring shouldn't have to "buy" her. In explaining its decision, the court likened Lerch to a defective cow and Gring to the man about to buy that cow. According to the court, "A man does not contract to marry a woman for the mere pleasure of paying for her board and washing. He expects and is entitled to something in return, and if the woman with whome he contracts be incapable by reason of a natural impediment of giving him the comfort and satisfaction to which as a married man he would be entitled, then there is a failure of the moving consideration of such contract . . ."

Gring showed how the marital bargain could come disturbingly close to treating wives as property. Still, in general, the language of economic exchange was beneficial to women. Discussing marriage in market terms acknowledged the reality of women's economic position and allowed courts to address women's relationship harms as monetary harms. Breach of promise cases, common-law marriage claims, and alimony suits were all based on this economic conception of marriage.

In breach of promise cases, courts held that engagements, like sale contracts, could not be broken without an economic penalty and applied the economic principles of caveat emptor (buyer beware / purchase at your own risk) to engagements. This economic conception of marriage meant most jilted fiancées were entitled to significant monetary compensation. It also meant these damages would increase when the failed engagement was to a wealthier man, as the courts recognized, in such cases, the financial loss was greater.

Women's common-law marriage claims similarly benefited from the law's economic view of marriage. Common-law marriages are marriages created through mutual consent, without a religious or legal ceremony. This informality can make their existence difficult to prove, but nineteenth-century courts solved this evidentiary problem by looking to the marital bargain. They held that when women provided wifely services — childcare, housework, companionship, and so on

— they were "wives" and entitled to the financial benefits of marriage.

Alimony was the most obvious benefit of the economic conception of marriage. This was money paid to a wife (only wives could receive alimony) upon divorce or separation. It was based on the marital bargain's support obligation but applied to separated wives. Although these women were no longer providing their husbands with domestic services, courts held that the support obligation continued. By marrying, a woman gained the right to financial support for life.

The allure of lifetime support is apparent in many nineteenth-century matrimonial advertisements. Francesca Beauman, a historian of such ads, describes them as "blatant in this regard." According to Beauman, female advertisers would indicate their desire for a moneyed partner with terms like "in easy pecuniary circumstances," "industrious," "good trade and permanent income," "cultivated gentleman," and "good home." Some of these advertisers were simply gold diggers, but many matrimonial ads reveal the writer's economic desperation. In one heartbreaking ad, "an American lady, 20 years of age" sought a husband because she was "anxious for a home of her own so she can give her little girl a good education." Notably, men were receptive to such requests. In fact, many male-authored matrimonial ads specifically emphasized the advertiser's willingness to provide economic support in exchange for marriage. In one typical ad, a thirty-two-year-old backwoodsman with a prosperous farm sought "a good girl, not over 25 years of age." In return for marriage with such a lady, the man offered to "pay all expenses, receive her thankfully, and use her well . . ."

For nineteenth-century women, marrying for money was a reasonable economic decision, but this did not make it an even exchange. The potential unfairness of the marital bargain is poignantly illustrated in the following 1876 letter written to the editor of a suffragette magazine explaining why the author could not attend the US centennial. She writes:

> Married in pioneer times a poor man, and by our joint efforts have made us a home worth several thousand dollars; have borne nine children, and took the whole care of them. Five are men grown, four of them voters. The first twenty years I did all my housework sewing, washing and mending, except a few weeks at the advent of the babies. For the last sixteen years have had help part time but have had from two to four grandchildren to care for the last three years, one of them a baby. And now I want to go to the Centennial and cannot command a sixpence for all my labor. Husband owns and controls everything and says we have nothing to spend for such foolishness. Have no more power than a child. Now if my labor has been of any value in dollars and cents, I want those dollars and cents to do as I please with. I feel like advising every woman not to do another day's labor unless she can be the owner of the value of it. All the property I possess in my own right is this pen and holder, a present from my brother in California.
>
> Signed,
> PEN HOLDER

Pen Holder's predicament was not unique. Whether wives benefited from the marital bargain depended primarily on the kindness and generosity of their husbands. Pen Holder's letter exemplifies the degrading nature of this economic dependence, and it was against this backdrop that a new solution to women's financial dependence was proposed — love.

Marrying for Love

Love became an important aspect of Western marriage during the sixteenth-century Protestant Reformation, but it did not become a *reason* to marry until much later. Even Martin Luther, whose loving marriage was held out as the ideal to be emulated, believed that "marrying for love was unsound." Instead, the marital decision was expected to be based on more practical considerations — like money. Then, in the mid-nineteenth century, these views began to change. Increasingly, women were advised to reject the economic conception of marriage and marry for love. Love, they were told, would help them to avoid the inequality of the marital bargain.

One early example of such advice appears in the popular anonymously authored novel *Belinda; or An Advertisement for a Husband*. The novel, published in Massachusetts in 1799, begins with the heroine, Belinda Blacket, pursuing the marital bargain. In a letter to her friend Louisa Lenox, Belinda writes that she is impatient to find a husband and has decided to place a matrimonial ad in the newspaper. She will offer her beauty and domestic skills in exchange for financial support. "Beauty," writes Belinda, "like any other mercantile commodity, is become an article of traffic in our daily prints; advertisements indiscriminately announce the bargain and sale of a lady's person, or a bale of silk; and direct the readers, whither they are to repair to treat for the affection of a lady with as little reserve as if she had been a hogshead of sugar, or any other common article of commerce." Belinda makes this statement approvingly, but Louisa is horrified. As the novel progresses, Belinda also adopts this view and eventually acknowledges that "the project I was engaged in was a ridiculous one." The novel ends with Belinda falling in love with a poor chaplain named Mr. Proby, who, in an Austen-like twist, becomes wealthy when he wins a long-contested inheritance battle shortly before their wedding.

In *Belinda*, the criticism of marrying for money is clear, yet gentle. By the mid-nineteenth century, the anxiety surrounding the marital bargain had increased significantly. In 1842, a British article widely circulated in the United States expressed dismay that couples were treating marriage as a "mercantile transaction" and lamented that "before long, the state of the hymenal market will be chronicled in newspapers, in common with the other commercial affairs of the day." In 1860, an article in *Vanity Fair* magazine expressed even greater dismay:

> Good people, buy your wives and husbands at the livery establishments as you would horses, dogs, etc. No more courting, flirting, bother, disappointment and wounded feelings. Step up to the office, examine the stock, take your pick, pay your money and drive to the parson. Hurrah for progress!

Novels from this period also reflect a growing animosity toward the marital bargain. Anthony Trollope's popular Phineas novels, published in the 1860s, in particular sought to terrify women into rejecting the marital bargain. In these novels, the heroine, Lady Laura, spurns love in order to marry a powerful and influential man. She is then subjected to horrific abuse and, finally, exile. The novel ends with an image of Laura as "worn out, withered, an old woman before her time." The warning to those who married for money was clear. Nevertheless, it wasn't fear that convinced most women to embrace the changing conception of marriage, it was hope.

A husband's love offered the possibility of equality in an inherently unequal relationship. As historian Elizabeth Abbott explains, "Romantic love was seen as the lifeline to a decent life,

Theodore Weld and Angelina Grimke.

a guarantee that in a patriarchal society, an otherwise vulnerable wife would be respectfully treated by her loving husband." The wedding of famed women's rights advocate and abolitionist Angelina Grimke to Theodore Weld exemplified this possibility. During their wedding vows, Weld acknowledged the unequal and unfair power the laws of the United States gave a husband over the person and property of his wife. He then promised he would never exercise this legal authority and instead swore the only influence he had over Grimke would come from love.

Women were increasingly expected to marry for love, but this created a problem for the millions of women who still depended on marriage for economic security. These women could not make love their primary criteria in choosing a husband. The

"Get thee behind me, (Mrs.) Satan!"

Free Love movement arose in response to this tension. The term *Free Love* referred to an absence of legal ties, not promiscuity. The movement was based on the belief that marriage corrupted love. Free Lovers sought to promote love by eliminating legal marriage and the gender inequality that forced women to marry for reasons other than love. Victoria Woodhull, the first woman to run for president, ran on the Free Love platform. She advocated for commitments based on love rather than economic or legal concerns. In her famous 1871 speech in New York City, Woodhull declared:

> I have an inalienable, constitutional and natural right to love whom I may, to love as long or as short a

period as I can; to change that love every day if I
please, and with that right neither you nor any law
you can frame have any right to interfere. And I have
the further right to demand a free and unrestricted
exercise of that right, and it is your duty not only to
accord it, but as a community, to see I am protected
in it.

Ultimately, the Free Love movement was unsuccessful, but its
argument — that money corrupted love — was influential. Once
love became the accepted purpose of marriage, rights based on
the economic conception of marriage needed to change. As a
result, relationship-based claims, such as breach of promise to
marry, were transformed from economic harms into emotional
harms. They were even relabeled "heart-balm" actions to indicate
they were a remedy for a broken heart rather than a financial
loss. This change allowed such claims to continue, but it also
made them much less effective. Courts that had previously been
comfortable ordering compensation for the economic effects of
a failed relationship now expressed indignation at paying for a
broken heart. Male defendants quickly took advantage of this
change in judicial attitudes.

Breach of promise defendants began to argue that economic
compensation corrupted the purity of marriage. In one such
action, an attorney named George Lawyer won his case by
arguing that "the maintenance of actions for the breach of the
marriage contract so belittles and degrades the relation itself that
the public is coming to look upon it as a matter of business alone
. . . The divine purpose is destroyed. The sacred institution has
acquired a cash equivalent, and all its relations are cheapened
and vulgarized." Once love became the only acceptable basis for
marriage, breach of promise defendants could portray themselves as the true victims and paint their accusers as heartless

James Dobie, *A Breach of Promise* (June 1885).

manipulators who sought to trap them in a loveless marriage.
The effectiveness of such tactics is illustrated in cases like the
1874 Illinois decision *Donnerschlog v. Behrens*.

In *Donnerschlog*, Amelia Donnerschlog sued her former fiancé,
Augustus Behrens, for breach of promise. Behrens didn't deny
the engagement or his decision to end it. Instead, he claimed he
was justified because Donnerschlog had wanted her mother to
live with them after marriage. According to Behrens, this would
have ruined his marital happiness because the mother was a
"lordly and unpleasant" woman who "insisted on feeding me too
much cabbage, a vegetable, I alway[s] dislike."

Traditionally, an annoying mother-in-law was no defense to a
breach of marriage claim. However, as marriage was reoriented
around love and personal fulfillment, such ridiculous excuses
became valid. Men like Behrens could portray themselves as
the real victims, and courts were frequently sympathetic to such
arguments. In *Donnerschlog*, Judge Robert Banyon also saw
himself as the victim of an overbearing mother-in-law who had

destroyed his marital happiness, and he had no difficulty dismissing Donnerschlog's suit. In fact, he congratulated Behrens for jilting her! After Behrens stated he would rather pay a fine than marry Donnerschlog, Banyon delivered the following judgment:

> Allow me to shake hands with you. I envy your firmness. There was a period in the life of this court . . . when it was in circumstances similar to yours. If it had had the moral courage which you possess, it would have saved about twenty-five years of misery and unhappiness. The alternative presented to this court was whether it would marry a young lady and her mother, or whether it would pay $125 in gold. The court was poor at the time. It was earning an unsatisfactory living at the restaurant business. It yielded. It took the young woman and mother-in-law and kept the $125. For a quarter of a century this court has regretted its hasty action. It is glad to meet a man who cherishes happiness more than he does money.

Then, in the coup de grâce, Banyon fined Donnerschlog $10 "for trying to bring a man into slavery to a mother-in-law."

Amelia Donnerschlog should have won her case. Behrens proposed and she accepted. More important, she made major sacrifices to marry him. The couple met in Germany and became engaged. Behrens then emigrated to America, and Donnerschlog waited for him while he established himself in Chicago. When he finally sent for her, she, and her presumably widowed and dependent mother, traveled halfway across the world to join him. However, after arriving in a strange country, far from friends and family, Behrens instructed her to "leave her old mother out in the cold." Understandably, Donnerschlog refused but, instead of recognizing the harm caused by Behrens's behavior, including the significant economic harm, the court sympathized with him and punished her.

Reorienting marriage around love hurt women's breach of promise actions. It also had a similarly detrimental effect on their common-law marriage claims. Once trapping a man into a loveless marriage was viewed as potentially worse than tricking a woman into providing domestic services (including sex) outside of marriage, common-law marriage claims became harder to prove. To win a common-law marriage claim, women increasingly needed to show that love, rather than domestic exchange, was the basis of the relationship. This created a problem. Unlike domestic services, affection could be faked. As a result, courts began treating common-law marriage claimants with suspicion.

In most common-law marriage cases, the courts' suspicions were unjustified. In fact, the women suspected of fraud were often the ones being exploited. *In re Baldwin's Estate* is one such example. The case was brought by a young woman named Lillian Ashley, who claimed to be the common-law wife of California millionaire Elias Baldwin. The court believed Ashley was lying and rejected her claim. However, it is far more likely that Baldwin was the liar.

Ashley met Baldwin in 1896 when she was twenty-three and he was sixty-five. Ashley knew Baldwin was rich, and there is little doubt that was his primary appeal. Still, it was Baldwin who deceived Ashley. According to her legal filings, Baldwin told Ashley he was divorced, was in love with her, and wanted to marry. Then, when she accepted his proposal, he convinced her to "marry" in secret by claiming his divorce was still recent and he wished to avoid the scandal of a quick remarriage. Ashley agreed to this request and, after their secret marriage, lived with him as his "wife." When she discovered he had lied about his divorce she left him, but it was too late; Ashley was pregnant. She then asked Baldwin for support, and he refused.

Elias "Lucky" Baldwin.

There are many reasons to believe Ashley's version of events. For starters, Ashley was willing to risk her reputation and void her subsequent marriage to pursue her common-law marriage claim. After leaving California, Ashley had returned east, remarried, and become a respected member of the Boston community. Her suit threatened that hard-won respectability. Nevertheless, that is not the only reason to believe Ashley's version of events. More revealing is the fact that Baldwin had a reputation for doing exactly the kinds of things Ashley accused him of doing.

Years earlier, before returning east, Ashley had sued Baldwin for seduction, and an article in the *Indianapolis Journal* noted that she was far from the first. According to the newspaper, "Baldwin has so many times been the object of similar suits that, as he says, he no longer worries about a little thing like that." Baldwin's defense to Ashley's seduction suit was that his reputation as a liar was so well known that no woman "would trust him." During the seduction trial, this nonchalant attitude so enraged Ashley's sister that she shot Baldwin in the head. Amazingly, he survived this assassination attempt, earning him the nickname "Lucky Baldwin." This moniker then replaced his previous nickname, "the gay deceiver," a reference to his penchant for lying to the women he was interested in pursuing. Tellingly, Ashley wasn't even the first pregnant girl he'd abandoned. As a young man, Baldwin had impregnated his cousin, and when she sued him for support, he had her committed to an insane asylum. None of these details are included in the court decision dismissing Ashley's common-law marriage claim. Instead, Ashley is portrayed as a liar, and the opinion concludes with the hope that her failed suit would be "the last of a most malodorous brood."

Both *Donnerschlog* and *Baldwin's Estate* show how the rise of the love match could harm women's economic claims. Nevertheless, in the early nineteenth century, most courts still viewed marriage as an economic marital bargain, despite finding it increasingly distasteful. The 1915 Iowa Supreme Court decision *Main v. Main* is typical of such treatment. *Main* concerned a request for alimony brought by Mrs. Main against her husband, John Main. Mrs. Main was a gold digger or, as Mr. Main's counsel called her, an "adventuress." One of Mr. Main's witnesses testified that Mrs. Main had admitted, "If there wasn't some money back of old John Main I wouldn't marry him." This testimony was unflattering, but the court also considered it irrelevant.

The Main marriage was a classic example of the marital bargain. Mrs. Main had married for money, and Mr. Main knew it. When the couple met, Mr. Main was sixty-two years old, twice divorced, and wealthy. He was also unattractive and a womanizer. The same witness who disparaged Mrs. Main also described the sixty-two-year-old Main as looking seventy. Nevertheless, he was an ardent pursuer of women. The court unflatteringly referred to him as a man who "sought the graces of other women with a fervor not altogether Platonic." Notably, his amorous pursuits had already gotten him sued at least once. When he met Mrs. Main, he was in the midst of defending a breach of promise lawsuit from an earlier love interest. Still, this previous romantic mishap did not stop him from eagerly pursuing the forty-two-year-old Mrs. Main.

The court described the Main marriage as a fair exchange: "Both knew from the start exactly what they wanted. She wanted a husband with money — or money with a husband. He wanted a wife to adorn his house." And it said the evidence presented at trial

> may show a lack of affection and lay bare the sordid motive which prompts marriages of the kind we have here to deal with, but it is otherwise irrelevant to the issue. The desire for a home and the comforts of wealth has been the controlling influence of many marriages, especially of those who have passed the bloom of youth, and it is not at all inconsistent with a faithful observance of all the duties and proprieties of the married state.

The court then granted Mrs. Main alimony and concluded its opinion by noting that women had the same right to marry for non-love reasons as men did. "Strategy and management in securing an eligible matrimonial partner is not the exclusive privilege of the man, and the game law of the state provides no closed season against the kind of 'trapping' of which appellant complains."

The *Main* court recognized that the marital bargain benefited both men and women. However, women's rights advocates increasingly rejected this conclusion. They feared that the harms of the marital bargain, with its emphasis on female dependency and domestic roles, outweighed the benefits. Although these advocates recognized that many women were still financially dependent on marriage, they believed this dependency would soon disappear. In the early 1900s, a handful of states had already granted women the vote, the national suffrage movement was gaining momentum, and women's job opportunities were increasing steadily. Consequently, these advocates believed the need for marital support would soon be replaced with economic opportunities and financial equality. Unfortunately, the rapid equality they envisioned did not materialize.

Throughout the 1920s, marriage remained most women's primary form of economic support — but now the small equality gains women had achieved were used against them. The New Jersey annulment action *Woodward v. Heichelbach* highlights the disconnect between women's purported equality and their continuing financial vulnerability. The case began in 1922, when Rhoda Woodward married Emile Heichelbach, believing he was a rich man. Heichelbach had encouraged this belief. During their courtship, he told Woodward he owned two cars, possessed a large bank account, and had a prestigious, well-paying job. He even showed her a bank book with $2,000 in savings. Sadly, it was all a lie. The bank book was borrowed, and the cars, the job, and the money were all fabrications. Heichelbach was broke. Two days after the wedding, Woodward discovered the truth, and she was furious.

Woodward had worked before her marriage, but it was almost certainly low-paid wage work. In the 1920s, few single women earned enough to support a family and even fewer were able to retain employment once married. Consequently, marrying a poor man could literally be ruinous. The *Heichelbach* court ignored this reality. Instead, it described Woodward as a "mature business woman," and implied she didn't need a husband for support. It then snarkily declared that since Woodward "certainly did not marry for love," she should have done a better job of investigating Heichelbach's finances. According to the court, it was not its responsibility to assist those "who make stupid contracts." The court also downplayed the significance of Heichelbach's financial deception. Instead of recognizing the potential life-altering effects of his lies, the court dismissed them as typical of any man intent on "the winning of a bride." The court wrote, "Under such circumstances a man always puts his best foot forward to impress the woman of his choice with his desirability as a mate." Heichelbach's lies were just "painting the lily."

Cases like *Heichelbach* showed that gender equality arguments could be turned against vulnerable women. Nevertheless, many women's rights advocates continued to argue that the best way to achieve gender equality was to reject any privileges or disabilities of their sex. As a result, condemning relationship-based protections, especially heart-balm actions, became an increasingly important part of the women's rights movement. A 1935 editorial in the *Christian Science Monitor* exemplified such reasoning. It stated, "Women now have the legal right to collect their own wages, enter into business contracts, own property in their own name and in general to provide for themselves independently of men. One way they can prove their equality is by not asking for the kind of protection breach-of-promise laws are meant to give." The same year, the National Women's Party also attacked gender-based privileges and claimed heart-balm suits "should be laughed out of court."

In 1935, Professor Harriet Daggett, one of the first female law professors in the US, described breach of promise as something that "at one time may have been a necessary . . . [but] now seems at times almost a travesty." *Chicago Tribune* columnist Antoinette Donnelly echoed these sentiments when she declared breach of promise "simply does not belong in an era in which women work alongside men as competitors," and

From the *Honolulu Advertiser*, Sunday, April 14, 1935.

feminist author Dorothy Dunbar Bromley described a breach of promise action as putting "a contract to marry on the same footing as a bargain for a horse or a bale of hay." However, it was Indiana state representative Roberta Nicholson, the only female representative in the Indiana legislature, who became the biggest proponent of anti-heart-balm legislation.

Nicholson claimed breach of promise suits must be eliminated because they were "based on a theory that is dead as a dodo, since the equality of the sexes has become an actuality." Despite such statements, it is inconceivable that Nicholson actually believed gender equality had been achieved. As one of the few female politicians of the period, she had firsthand experience with gender discrimination. In fact, years later she described her male colleagues' reactions to her proposed bill as "wasn't it cute of her. She's got a bill. She's going to introduce it just like a man. Isn't that darling?" Still, despite such experiences, Nicholson appears to have fully embraced the women's rights argument that gender-based rights were more harmful than helpful. When presenting her bill to eliminate breach of promise actions she stated, "Women do not demand rights . . . they earn them, and they ask no such privileges as these which are abolished in this bill."

By proclaiming sex equality a fait accompli, early-twentieth-century feminists like Nicholson denied the continuing disparities between men and women, including the fact that most women still needed to rely on marriage for financial support. One result of this tactic was that the traditional economic protections of marriage — alimony, breach of promise, or common-law marriage — were increasingly viewed as unnecessary and the women who sought these benefits were attacked as "parasites," "harlots," and "bandits." These negative perceptions were then further fueled by intense and sensationalized media coverage.

During the 1930s, the frequency of heart-balm actions declined significantly, but the media coverage of these suits exploded. Between 1916 and 1920, the *Chicago Daily Tribune* published only thirty-nine stories referencing "alienation of affections" (a heart-balm suit based on the "stealing" of a spouse's love). Between 1921 and 1925, this number increased to 56; between 1926 and 1930, it rose to 102; and between 1931 and 1935, the paper published 230 stories, a nearly sixfold increase in coverage. Many of the most publicized heart-balm cases involved celebrities.

One famous alienation of affections claim involved the movie star Douglas Fairbanks, husband of actress Joan Crawford. In 1933, Fairbanks was sued by Jorgen Dietz for allegedly having an affair with Dietz's wife. The allegations were unsupported and untrue. In fact, they were deliberately manufactured by Fairbanks's movie studio to quell homosexuality rumors. Nevertheless, the public was unaware of these machinations, and when Fairbanks agreed to pay the Dietzes $50,000, it seemed like Fairbanks was being exploited.

From the *Independent Record* (Helena, Montana), Sunday, October 18, 1931.

Cases such as Fairbanks's fostered the inaccurate perception that the financial abuse of men was a serious problem. This led to the elimination of most heart-balm laws but also, increasingly, common-law marriage. The 1932 New York common-law marriage case *In re Estate of Erlanger* highlighted the changing acceptance of laws that had once supported and encouraged the marital bargain.

Charlotte Fixel-Erlanger was a beautiful former Broadway actress who claimed to be the common-law wife of Abraham Erlanger, a wealthy, much older Broadway producer. The couple had lived together for decades but had never formally married. When Erlanger died, Fixel-Erlanger sought recognition as his wife and the beneficiary of his estate. Her claim was based on the marital bargain. She was a wife, she argued, because she performed wifely services. She had lived with Erlanger, traveled with him, and cared for him. In return, she had received, and depended on, Erlanger's financial support. One of her lawyer's earliest arguments was that "every department store in New York has charge accounts in the name Mrs. Erlanger." Spending

Erlanger's money — she regularly ordered his food, clothes, and
housewares — was presented as evidence of marriage. As Fixel-
Erlanger's lawyers explained in their briefs, "Wives do select
suits for their husbands, but mistresses do not. Such conduct
bespeaks the attention and life of a housewife, and not the life
of a wanton."

Very different arguments were made by the lawyers for
Erlanger's estate. They suggested that the financial benefits
Fixel-Erlanger received from her relationship with Erlanger
made her more like a prostitute than a wife. Throughout the
trial, the estate's arguments focused on Fixel-Erlanger's alleged
mercenary motives and her presumed lack of affection for
Erlanger. One witness testified to an incident in which Fixel-
Erlanger nagged Erlanger to purchase a diamond-and-gold
wristwatch for her and then confided to the witness, "I got to
get it while the getting is good." A different witness testified
that Fixel-Erlanger didn't love Erlanger and just wanted "what
she could get out of him," adding, "she would buy an automobile
as you would buy cigarettes." Other witnesses made even more
damning accusations. One described Fixel-Erlanger as "a very
bad woman . . . a dangerous woman" and warned, "If anything
happens to me, and don't forget this, whatever she says about me
is what she has manufactured." Another claimed Fixel-Erlanger
had wanted Erlanger dead so badly she had even planned her
funeral outfit, "a white coat . . . trimmed with white fox fur and
her emeralds." Together, these witnesses painted Fixel-Erlanger
as a heartless gold digger who did not love Erlanger and thus
could not be his wife.

Ultimately, the court ignored the attacks on Fixel-Erlanger's
character and ruled in her favor, but the court knew its decision was controversial. Tellingly, the court's 500-page opinion
included specifics "of every encounter, every document, every
conversation, every purchase, every dinner, every disagreement,

From the *Courier-News* (Bridgewater, New Jersey), 1932.

and every excursion." As law professor Ariela Dubler explains, the judge recognized "his decision would be a controversial one." In fact, the public was outraged. Most Americans believed Fixel-Erlanger had never loved Erlanger and didn't deserve to inherit his wealth. When she remarried shortly after her legal victory, this perception was seemingly confirmed. It is likely no coincidence that within months of the *Erlanger* decision, New York joined the growing list of states outlawing common-law marriage.

Erlanger was decided during the midst of the Great Depression. Money was scarce, and an extra mouth to feed could cause real financial hardship. Most single women lived at home, and with few economic opportunities, many were burdens on their families. Consequently, despite the widespread criticism of gold digging, marrying for money remained an important survival tool for many women and their families. Occasionally, this reality was acknowledged.

Joan Blondell and Guy Kibbee in *Gold Diggers of 1933*.

In the shooting script for the movie *Gold Diggers of 1933*, there is a scene in which a beautiful young woman is embraced by a much older man after having just accepted his marriage proposal. Moments later, she receives a call that she has been hired as a chorus girl. The woman hangs up the phone, smiles, breaks free of the embrace, slaps the man, and leaves. The implication is that the woman only agreed to marriage because she had no other financial options. As soon as she is offered a well-paying job, she loses all interest in marrying for money. Economic anxiety, not greed, was the key thing keeping her in the relationship and making her feign affection for a man she detested.

Throughout the 1930s, women lacked meaningful economic alternatives to marriage, but this changed dramatically when America entered World War II. For the first time, significant numbers of American women were eligible for well-paying

A Department of Defense photo of women shipfitters working on board the USS *Nereus* at the US Navy Yard in Mare Island, circa 1943.

jobs and could support themselves. Suddenly, women didn't need to marry for money. American men should have been thrilled. Tellingly, they were not. Women's potential economic independence made men fearful. Without a financial need for marriage, many worried that women might no longer choose to marry. Returning American soldiers repeatedly cited this fear as the reason they wed foreign brides. As one such soldier explained, "I don't know whether I am going to have a job when I get back. I don't know how things will be with me. Maybe I couldn't make an American girl happy with what I have to offer her." Another simply said, "American women demand so much more."

For centuries, female economic dependence had enhanced men's marriage prospects and made even poor providers appear relatively attractive. Without this economic incentive, many men worried their marital prospects were no longer as promising.

The gender equality of the war years was short-lived, however. When World War II ended, the need to employ returning soldiers forced most women to abandon their wartime careers. They returned to the home and the marital bargain. As a result, women's need to marry for money did not end in the 1940s. Nor did it end in the twentieth century. Even today, continuing gender inequality means marrying for money remains many women's best financial option. However, money is far from the only non-love reason Americans marry. Before returning to a contemporary examination of gold digging, the following chapters will explore other equally important, but less well-known, motivations that have long convinced Americans to marry for reasons other than love.

chapter two

The Government Loves a Gold Digger

Politics doesn't make strange bedfellows — marriage does.

— GROUCHO MARX

In 1835, when Esther Sumner was twenty-one, she married Noah Damon, a seventy-five-year-old Revolutionary War veteran. It was not a love match. Esther married Noah because she believed he was wealthy; she quickly learned he was broke. In fact, he needed her to support him. For one year, Esther and Noah lived on her small teacher's salary. Then Esther tired of this arrangement and sent Noah to live with his grown children. The couple never lived together again, and the marriage appeared to be a financial disaster. However, when Noah died, Esther became eligible for a widow's pension. She received this pension until her death at age ninety-three. Her once worthless marriage had entitled her to decades of government support.

LAST WIDOW OF REVOLUTION.

Mrs Esther Sumner Damon, Cousin of Charles Sumner, Died Yesterday at Plymouth Union, Vt.

MRS ESTHER SUMNER DAMON.

In 1836, one year after the Damons married, Congress passed the Widows' Pension Act and began paying pensions to the wives of military veterans. Initially, the act applied only to women who married prior to their husbands' military service, but over time it expanded to include those who married later. This change meant women could now marry for pensions, and many quickly recognized the financial advantages of such marriages. If a young woman wed an older veteran, marriage could mean a lifetime of government support. Alberta Martin, one of the last Confederate widows, was motivated by such economic incentives.

In 1927, when Alberta was twenty-one, she married William Jasper Martin, an eighty-one-year-old Civil War veteran. A 2003 *Baltimore Sun* article on the Martin marriage described it as blatantly mercenary, writing, "he was lonely, she was needy" and his "$50-a-month military pension [was] a princely sum in those days for a woman who staked her whole life by poverty." The article further emphasized the transactional nature of Alberta's marriage, and her presumed lack of affection for William, by noting that less than eight weeks after William's death she married his grandson. According to the article's author, this scandalous second marriage "set so many tongues wagging in town that the local Baptist preacher had to study the Scriptures before deciding she hadn't committed a sin."

The marriage of Helen Viola Jackson, the last official Civil War widow, was even more explicitly transactional. In 1936, when Jackson was seventeen, she married ninety-three-year-old Civil War veteran James Bolin. Jackson met Bolin when her father sent her over to help with Bolin's chores. Bolin lacked the money to pay but offered to marry Jackson instead. Recognizing the economic benefits of such a marriage, she agreed. "He said that he would leave me his Union pension. It was during the [Great] Depression and times were hard. He said that it might be my only way of leaving the farm."

Critics of the Widows' Pension Act recognized that the law could encourage mercenary marriages. In 1843, during the debates on the act's reauthorization, Massachusetts senator Rufus King

William Jasper Martin (left), a Civil War veteran who married a woman sixty years younger than himself, and his widow, Alberta Martin (above).

urged his fellow lawmakers to reject the act because it could benefit gold diggers. He asked his fellow lawmakers: "What merit [i]s there in these women marrying officers and soldiers of the Revolution after the war, that they should be entitled to pensions? Go to the Pension Office, and you will find that most of these widows who had married those old revolutionary officers, soon after their deaths provided themselves with young husbands."

King's concerns were valid yet were largely dismissed. Widows' pensions were popular, and the women who received them, even the gold diggers, were widely viewed as deserving. These women had provided marital services to their veteran husbands; thus, under the terms of the marital bargain, they were entitled to compensation. Senator Perry Smith of Connecticut employed such reasoning when he voiced his support for the act's reauthorization, "not on the ground of a gratuity, but because the females of that day were all more or less compelled to make sacrifices and had besides rendered material services." In 1850, Representative

Illustration by Keppler and Schwarzmann, 1898.

Abraham Venable of North Carolina echoed these sentiments when he explained that the purpose of a widow's pension was "to give to the widow something, some compensation for the years of anxiety and care spent over her husband who fell under the effects of . . . wounds received in the service."

The pension act was characterized as a continuation of the husband's support duty, and this allowed it to avoid Congress's normally strong condemnation of public charity. It also helped lawmakers dismiss the concerns of critics like Senator King. In the nineteenth century, women were expected to marry for support; widows' pensions were treated as just another form of marital support.

In 1864, the Civil War pension statute extended pensions to the widows of "colored soldiers." It also adopted a generous and easily provable definition of marriage. The act stated that in cases where the "husband" of a newly freed woman was killed during the Civil War, the widow and her children were allowed to receive a pension for the soldier without proof of legal marriage. The alleged wife was simply required to show the couple "had habitually recognized each other as man and wife, and lived together as such." In 1873, pensions were also extended to widows of "Indian soldiers and sailors" who had cohabited for at least two years and recognized "each other as man and wife."

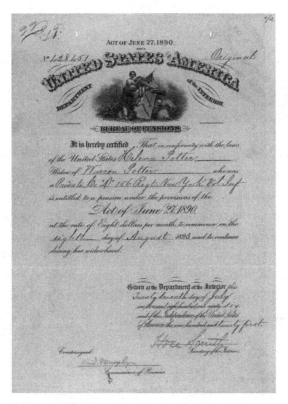

Authorization of a pension petition, August 1893.

By the 1890s, widows' pensions were supporting hundreds of thousands of women and children and accounted for nearly half the federal budget. These funds provided valuable support to needy women, but they were not without drawbacks. Widows' pensions conditioned government support on marriage and, in doing so, ignored the needs of other impoverished women. Single women were ineligible for government support; they were simply instructed to marry. This was not the only problem with conditioning government benefits on marriage. Linking benefits to marriage could create dangerous and even deadly incentives. The Oregon Donation Land Act of 1850 exposed this potential peril.

The Oregon Donation Land Act

Initially, marital status was irrelevant to Oregon land claims. Both single and married male settlers were permitted to claim 640-acre plots. Then, the Donation Land Act went into effect, and land eligibility changed. Suddenly, single men were entitled to only half the amount available to married men. Men living in Oregon prior to December 1, 1850, were entitled to 320 acres if they were single, or 640 acres if they were married. Similarly, for settlers arriving after December 1, 1850, a male claimant could receive 160 acres of land if he was single, or 320 acres if he was married. In both instances, the second parcel of land would be in the wife's name, but since the husband typically controlled his wife's land parcel, marriage effectively doubled his acreage.

The Donation Land Act's preference for married settlers reflected the well-established view that marriage facilitated homesteading. In 1838, when Iowa was the western frontier, a correspondent for the *Dubuque Iowa News* joked, "So anxious are our settlers for wives that they never ask a single lady her age.

All they require is *teeth.*" The 1846 *Emigrant's Guide to Iowa* made a similar, albeit less humorous, observation, noting, "Married persons are generally more comfortable, and succeed better, in a frontier country, than single men; for a wife and family, so far from being a burden to a western farmer, may always prove a source of pecuniary advantage in the domestic economy of his household."

Wives made homesteading easier. They also made frontier communities more stable. Census figures indicate that single men were more transient than married men. For example, the 1850 census records from Wapello County, Iowa, showed that 91 percent of single men had left since the previous census, while only 73 percent of those with families had departed. Similarly, an 1860 census from Roseburg, Oregon, revealed that only one-third of single men stayed more than five years, while approximately two-thirds of married men remained. Given such significant differences, many western politicians eagerly sought to incentivize female immigration. In 1850, Samuel R. Thurston, the Oregon Territory's congressional delegate, was so eager for female settlers that he asked Congress to provide them with immigration incentives. He wrote:

> Emigrating to Oregon from the States, places the female beyond the reach of her kindred and former friends; and it is certainly no more than right to place some little means of protection in her own hands. But the object is to produce a population, and this provision is an encouragement of the women to peril the dangers and hardships of the journey.

In response to Thurston's request, Congress passed the Donation Land Act and guaranteed female homesteaders a parcel of land in their own name and as a separate estate. This

Samuel R. Thurston.

was the first time the government had permitted married women to own government land, and it was a significant immigration incentive. However, it was an even stronger incentive for those already living in the Oregon Territory to marry. In the July 29, 1851, issue of the *Oregon Spectator*, the paper's editors noted the marital benefit of the act and encouraged Oregon's singles to wed before the December 1 deadline:

> The first day of December 1851 is near at hand. Your days of grace soon expire, and the 320 acres lost beyond redemption, unless you are up and stirring. The ladies, it seems to us, should wear their most winning smiles, and encourage the timid young man to nerve himself up to the sticking point, and boldly declare his desire to possess another half [section].

The article implies that the primary impediment to marriage was male nerves. However, the true problem was numbers. White women were scarce in Oregon, and demand far exceeded supply. In 1849, women accounted for fewer than 20 percent of travelers on the Oregon Trail, and in 1850, when the Donation Land Act was passed, male settlers outnumbered female settlers by a ratio of 2.5 to 1. In some counties, the ratio was almost 4 to 1. There were simply not enough women to marry. As a result, many land-hungry men turned to teenagers and even children.

Oregon settler Jennie Stevenson Miller described the marital frenzy of her childhood, stating: "I had my first offer of marriage when I was 13, and from then till I was 24 I had numerous proposals." Miller resisted these offers because, as she explained, "I had a pretty strong suspicion that many of the men who wanted to marry me wanted the extra land they could get if they were married." Still, countless other girls accepted, or were forced to accept, these proposals. Abigail Scott Duniway, editor of Oregon's first women's rights newspaper, wrote about the child marriages the Land Donation Act had incentivized and highlighted the abuse inherent in these relationships. According to Duniway, "When a man of forty, thirty or even twenty-five marries a child of fourteen . . . the result is subjugation on one hand and despotism upon the other." Oregon settler Elvina Apperson Fellows was the victim of such abuse. She had married as a young teen, and her husband beat her regularly. Years later, she recounted: "[He] used to beat me until I thought I couldn't stand it." She also noted she had little recourse to stop the abuse. "What could a girl of 14 do, to protect herself from a man of 44?" Some older husbands even considered the ability to abuse an added benefit of child marriage. Oregon homesteader George Bennett once remarked to a neighbor that his wife, Lureana, "gave herself to him when she was but a child," and as a result, he "had had her under his thumb ever since — he could use her just as he pleased."

The law of coverture already left wives vulnerable to abuse and exploitation. Laws incentivizing men to marry women they didn't love, and maybe didn't even like, further increased this risk. Intermarriages between white men and Indian women provide some of the most tragic examples.

White Men Preying on Native Women

By the mid-nineteenth century, Indian tribes had been deprived of millions of acres of ancestral lands. However, many still retained significant, and often desirable, landholdings. When these lands were not for sale, marriage became an effective means for non-Native men to gain ownership. The 1848 case *Wells v. Thompson* set the precedent for such land grabs.

In 1821, Mary Wells, a Creek woman, married a white man named William Wells. Initially, the couple lived within the boundaries of Creek Nation. In 1828, the Wells family left Creek territory and moved to Alabama. Shortly thereafter, William abandoned Mary for another woman, and Mary and her children returned to her father's home in Creek Nation. Four years later, the tribe signed the 1832 Treaty of Cusseta. Under this treaty, Creek Nation relinquished rights to all land east of the Mississippi. In return, the head of each family received a land allotment. Mary received one of these parcels, but after her death, William claimed the land as his own.

The Wells children contested William's claim. They argued that according to Creek custom, Mary had divorced William by returning to her father's home. Thus, because Mary and William were divorced before she received her allotment, William had no right to the land. The Alabama Supreme Court rejected this argument. It held that because the separation did not occur on Indian land, the marriage could not be dissolved by Creek custom and that William remained head of the family and was entitled to the allotted lands.

Wells demonstrated that marriage to an Indian woman could provide white men with rights to Indian lands. Then, the 1854 Mississippi case *Turner v. Fish* confirmed this benefit of marriage. In *Fish*, a white man named Freeman J. Smith claimed a treaty right to Choctaw land. Under the Treaty of Dancing Rabbit, an allotment of Choctaw land was given to the head of each Choctaw family. Smith argued that because he was married to a Choctaw woman and living within the Choctaw Nation, he was the head of a Choctaw family. The Mississippi Supreme Court agreed. The court acknowledged that "the treaty has reference to the head of a family living under the dominion of the Choctaw nation" but noted that "the treaty does not say that a white man may not according to the usages and customs of that nation, be the head of the family." Therefore, the court found that Smith was "head" of a Choctaw family. In reaching this decision, the court dismissed Choctaw matrilineal custom recognizing women as heads of family and declared it could "only take judicial notice of the law . . . It can take no judicial notice of local custom." As a result, Smith gained control of his wife's tribal allotment. He then immediately sold the land and pocketed the profits. His wife and children received nothing.

Marriage could be an effective means of gaining Indian lands, and many white men took advantage of this strategy. By 1874, the problem of marrying for Indian land had become so problematic in Cherokee territory that the Cherokee Nation passed a statute declaring that, in light of the "rapidly growing value of Cherokee lands . . . [the] rights and privileges herein conferred through intermarriage shall not extend to a right of soil or interest in the vested funds of this Nation." The problem of marrying for Indian land was also vividly illustrated by the rapid amendment of the 1887 Dawes Act, which had inadvertently incentivized such marriages.

The purpose of the Dawes Act was to break up Indian land-holdings in the West and open these lands to white settlement. The act divested Native American tribes of nearly ninety million acres, or approximately two-thirds of their lands. Nevertheless, even after allotment, a significant portion of lands remained reserved for tribes and tribal citizens. These were valuable lands, and to prevent tribal members from being threatened or swindled out of these remaining parcels, the act included a twenty-five-year ban on their sale. This provision ensured that non-Indians could not buy allotted Indian lands — but it did nothing to prevent them from marrying for these lands. Within a year, Congress recognized it had made a grave mistake. It then passed a second statute clarifying that white men who married Indian women could not, by virtue of the marriage, acquire "any right to any tribal property, privilege, or interest whatever to which any member of such tribe is entitled."

After the Dawes Act was amended, white men could no longer marry for tribal lands. However, marriage still gave them access to the reservations and their resources, and this could be almost as valuable. White men suspected of marrying Native women for access to tribal resources were dubbed squaw men. This was a pejorative term, and such husbands were generally seen as disreputable and even dangerous. In the August 16, 1889, Commissioner of Indian Affairs Report, Thomas Priestley of the Yakima Agency wrote, "The white men who marry Indian women for purposes of getting a home on an Indian reservation are not of the better class." In the August 11, 1890, report, Hal J. Cole of the Colville Agency noted that such men are "of the lower class . . . Nine out of every ten are addicted to whisky drinking or else they have some other pernicious habit and their presence on the reservation does the Indians harm instead of

Indian agent V. T. McGillycuddy.

good." And in the September 18, 1890, report, Webster L. Stabler
of the Yakima Agency described "the squaw-men . . . [as] a
constant menace to the welfare of the Indians."

Indian agents tended to focus the on the problems caused
by white husbands' drinking and gambling, but it was resource
grabbing that was often the biggest threat to the welfare of the
tribe. In the late nineteenth century, intermarriage had enabled
white men to dominate the cattle ranching industry on the
Pine Ridge Reservation of South Dakota. Although the reservation and its grazing lands were intended to be off limits to
white ranchers, marriage provided a lucrative exception. In 1880,
Indian agent V. T. McGillycuddy lamented the advantages
these white ranchers gained from intermarriage, writing, "The
squaw-men assume that by marriage they have all the rights of
full-blooded Indians, and they endeavor to exercise these rights
not only in possession of cattle themselves, but also in ranging
and pasturing upon Indian reservations large herds belonging to

other white men." As McGillycuddy noted, once white ranchers had access to reservation resources, their connections and
understanding of the American ranching industry gave them an
unparalleled advantage over their Indian competitors.

In 1893, a *Harper's Magazine* article about the Native nations
of Oklahoma specifically highlighted the financial benefits
white husbands gained from intermarriage. The article noted
that in Cherokee Nation, "a Cherokee squaw man . . . is said to
hold more land than is held by all the full-bloods of the tribe."
It also reported that "a score of Chickasaw citizens, in whom
combined there is hardly enough blood to make a full-blood
Indian, control nearly ninety percent of the arable lands of that
nation." By 1908, the practice of marrying Indian women for
their land was so common in Oklahoma that, when the *Taylor-
Trotwood Magazine* published an article extolling the virtues
of the new state, it openly advised the arriving male settlers to

Beaver Dick Leigh, 1872, with his first wife, Jenny, a Shoshone of Washakie's
band, and their children. The marriage of Leigh and Jenny appears to have
been a love match. After she died, Leigh named Jenny Lake, one of the most
beautiful lakes in the Tetons, in her honor.

A delegation from the council of the Osage Indian tribe of Oklahoma travels to Washington, DC, to take up the question of leasing oil lands in the Osage reservation.

marry Indian wives. According to the article's author, an Indian wife "is a thing of beauty and a joy forever, and she and each of her sisters has a great big farm."

Some white husbands undoubtedly loved their native wives. Tragically, many did not. The Osage murders of Oklahoma are one particularly chilling example of the dangers of linking government benefits to marriage. In 1906, Congress passed the Osage Allotment Act, dividing approximately 1.5 million acres of land among the members of the Osage Nation. It also placed the mineral interest for these lands in trust for the Osage and provided that all funds due to the tribe would be divided pro rata among the individual tribal members or their heirs. These shares were known as headrights, and when oil was discovered on Osage land, those eligible for headrights became, at least in theory, enormously wealthy.

The problem was that full-blooded Osage Indians were considered "incompetent" to manage their vast oil wealth. As a result, they were assigned financial guardians. These "guardians" were typically prominent white residents of Osage County, who were granted near-total control over the finances of their Osage wards. Nearly all of these men were corrupt. Many trustees concocted complex transactions to swindle their Osage wards. Others just robbed them outright. There was little the Osage could do to prevent this abuse; the one exception was marriage. An Osage woman could avoid financial guardianship by marrying a white man. This husband would then be permitted to take the place of the government-appointed guardian. Through marriage, an Osage woman could potentially avoid the corrupt guardians determined to steal her money. Sadly, marriage often turned out to be infinitely worse. The Kyle family was particularly unlucky in this regard.

In 1919, Ernest Burkhart married Mollie Kyle for her headrights. Headrights could not be bought or sold, but they could be inherited. Therefore, at the urging of his uncle and brother, Ernest wed Mollie and helped carry out a plan to murder her and her family. Mollie's sister Ana was killed first. She was shot in the back of the head, but her death was staged to look alcohol related. Shortly after Ana's murder, Lizzie Kyle, Mollie's mother, was poisoned. Then a bomb was placed under the house of Mollie's sister Rita. Both Rita and her husband were killed. Chillingly, Mollie and Ernest's children were supposed to be in the house when the bomb exploded. They were spared by a last-minute illness. Finally, after murdering Ana, Lizzie, and Rita, Ernest began poisoning Mollie. She became gravely ill, but by that time the newly formed FBI was investigating the Kyle family murders and uncovered the plan to kill Mollie. As a result, she survived.

Mollie Kyle and her sisters.

Ernest Burkhart, his brother, and his uncle were all convicted of murder. However, the Kyle murders were not isolated acts. Many white men were willing to marry and murder Osage women for headrights. In fact, Burkhart wasn't even the first husband to murder a Kyle sister. Before Ernest married Mollie, a white man named Bill Smith had married a fourth sister, Minnie Kyle, who died of a mysterious wasting disease shortly after their marriage. Then, after Minnie's death, Bill married her sister Rita and presumably would have murdered her, too, except Ernest killed her (and Bill) first.

Despite the tragic outcome, it is understandable why Mollie and her sisters chose white husbands: Intermarriage gave the Kyle sisters a chance to circumvent the racist laws denying them access to valuable government benefits. As the twentieth century progressed, this use of marriage became increasingly common. Thousands of immigrants used marriage to circumvent the racist, sexist, and xenophobic laws enacted to exclude them. This became a common non-love reason for couples to marry, but such marriages could also lead to abuse and exploitation.

Immigration's Marriage Loophole

Initially, neither citizenship law nor immigration regulations had any relationship to marriage. In the 1830 case *Shanks v. Dupont*, the Supreme Court held that "marriage with an alien . . . produces no dissolution of the native allegiance of the wife." *Shanks* concerned the citizenship of Ann Shanks, a US citizen who had married a British officer and then fled with him to Britain during the Revolutionary War. Years later, her heirs sought to reclaim the land she had possessed before the war, and the ownership issue turned on Shanks's citizenship. If Shanks was an American citizen, then she had abandoned and forfeited her property when she fled to Britain. However, if she was a British citizen, then the land had been captured and, under the peace treaty between the US and Britain, must be returned. After considering the issue, the court held that Shanks was a British subject because she moved to Britain and voluntarily "chose to live under British protection," but not because of her marriage. In the words of Justice Story, "The incapacities of femes covert . . . apply to their civil rights, and are for their protection and interest. But they do not reach their political rights, nor prevent their acquiring or losing a national character."

Twenty-five years later, in 1855, Congress rejected the *Shanks* court's reasoning and passed a statute automatically naturalizing the wife of a US citizen. The new law clarified that women's citizenship, like most of their other legal rights, was affected by marriage and that foreign wives would share the citizenship of their American husband. As Representative Francis Cutting of New York explained when arguing in favor of the act, married women "possess no political rights . . . [therefore], where you confer on her the political character of her husband, it is a relief to the husband, it aids him in the instilling of proper principles in his children and cannot interfere with any possible right of a political character."

In some ways, the new martial citizenship law was very broad. For example, it included wives who had never even set foot in the US. In other ways, it was extremely limited. The law only applied to women who could "lawfully be naturalized under existing laws," which meant it only applied to white wives. After the Civil War, some of the racial bars on naturalization were removed. In 1870, persons "of African descent or nativity" were permitted to naturalize. Then, in 1888, American Indian wives of white men also became eligible for naturalization. However, neither of these amendments applied to Asian immigrants. They remained ineligible for naturalization. As a result, marriage could not confer citizenship on Asian wives. Nevertheless, as America's anti-Asian immigration restrictions expanded in the late nineteenth century, marriage became an important strategy for avoiding these exclusionary laws.

Asian Exclusion Acts

The first Asian exclusion law was the 1875 Page Act, which prohibited the entry of involuntary "Oriental" labor, prostitutes, and others coming for "lewd and immoral purposes." The Page Act was followed by the 1882 Chinese Exclusion Act, which barred Chinese laborers from entering the US. Shortly thereafter, immigration officials interpreted the act as also preventing the wives of Chinese laborers from entering the country. In 1884, Too Cheong, a Chinese laborer living in the United States, challenged the act as a violation of his marital rights.

Too Cheong had traveled to China and married a woman named Ah Moy. The couple then returned to the United States, but after the passage of the exclusion act. Upon arrival, Ah Moy

Exclusion act, 1882. *The Only One Barred Out.*

was imprisoned and ordered deported. Too Cheong then challenged this deportation order. He argued that Ah Moy's exclusion violated the terms of the 1880 treaty with China, which
stated that "Chinese laborers who are now in the United States,
shall be allowed to go and come of their own free will and accord,
and shall be accorded all the rights, privileges, immunities, and
exemptions which accorded to the citizens and subjects of the
most favor." According to Too Cheong, this provision guaranteed him the right to his wife's company and companionship.
The court disagreed.

   The *Ah Moy* court conceded that a wife's companionship was
one of the essential rights of marriage but held that the exclusion act had limited this right. As the court explained, a wife
assumed the immigration status of her husband and therefore,
because Too Cheong was a Chinese laborer, Ah Moy was also a
Chinese laborer. The court held that marriage did not create an

THROWING DOWN THE LADDER BY WHICH THEY ROSE.

Throwing Down the Ladder by Which They Rose by Thomas
Nast, July 23, 1870.

exception to the exclusion act. As a result, Too Cheong lost, but
other Chinese husbands were more successful.

In 1899, the US Supreme Court decided *U.S. v. Gue*. Gue Lim
was the wife of a Chinese merchant named Fook Kee. In 1887,
the couple traveled from China to Tacoma, Washington, and
initially both Gue and Fook were granted entry based on Fook's
status as a Chinese merchant. Five months later, the collector of
customs changed his mind and charged Gue Lim with unlaw-
ful entry. She was imprisoned and ordered deported. Fook Kee
then sued for her release. Like Too Cheong, Fook argued that as
Gue's husband, he had the right to her care and companionship
and that as the wife of a Chinese merchant, Gue's entry was not
barred by the exclusion argument.

In its brief to the US Supreme Court, the government
conceded that marriage gave Gue Lim the right to enter the

THE CHINESE QUESTION AGAIN.

The Chinese Question Again. Chinese Exclusion in New
Jersey: Immigration Law in the Past and Present.

US as a wife of an admissible immigrant. It wrote, "The United
States at the outset disclaims any intention to contend against
the fundamental and natural right of the valid wife and legitimate minor children of Chinese merchants, not being laborers, to come and remain in this country." The problem, claimed
the government, was not that wives of Chinese merchants were
ineligible for entry, but that Gue had failed to file the correct
paperwork prior to arrival. This was a weak and disingenuous
argument (the supposedly required forms were not even obtain-
able outside the United States), and the court quickly rejected it.

Consequently, *Gue* confirmed that merchant wives could "enter by reason of the right of the husband and without the certificate mentioned in the Act of 1884."

In 1902, in *Tsoi Sim v. U.S.*, the court confirmed the marital immigration exception also applied to the wives of second-generation Chinese Americans. Tsoi Sim was a Chinese woman who had entered the United States a few months before the passage of the exclusion act. Twenty years later, on April 20, 1901, she was arrested for being a female laborer of Chinese descent. At the time of her arrest, Tsoi was married to Yee Yuk, a US citizen by birth. Therefore, Tsoi Sim argued, she should be treated as the wife of a native-born citizen and not as an inadmissible laborer. Tsoi's arguments focused on the sanctity of the marital relation and on "the right of the citizen husband to have and enjoy the society and company of whomsoever he may lawfully marry." Tsoi's attorneys described this right as one of the most fundamental rights of citizenship and argued that if Tsoi Sim was deported, "the founders of our great Republic [will have] fought and bled in vain, and our boasted 'liberty of the citizen' is but an idle dream." The court agreed. It held that marriage had changed Tsoi's status "from that of a Chinese laborer to that of wife of a native-born citizen." It then confirmed that as a wife, Tsoi had the right "to live with her husband; enjoy his society; receive his support and maintenance and all the comforts and privileges of the marriage relations."

Gue Lim and *Tsoi Sim* showed that marriage could be used to circumvent Chinese immigration restrictions. Marriage was an even more successful means of avoiding restrictions on Japanese immigration. In 1907, Japan and the US signed the Gentleman's Agreement. This agreement banned nearly all Japanese immigration to the United States but made an exception for the wives of Japanese men already residing in the US. Although these men could not leave the United States to find wives, they could marry

Picture brides wait to meet their new husbands.

by proxy and then send for their wives to join them. The arriving women were known as picture brides, because their American husbands had only seen their photographs. Between 1908 and 1920, more than ten thousand Japanese women used this exception to enter the United States.

Barring "Immoral Women"

The Chinese Exclusion Act and the Gentleman's Agreement affected only Asian immigrants, but other "undesirable" immigrants were also targeted by America's growing immigration restrictions. In 1882, Congress enacted legislation to bar "lunatic[s]," "idiot[s]," and "any person unable to take care of himself or herself without becoming a public charge" from entry into the United States. Shortly thereafter, it amended the phrase "without becoming a public charge" to "likely to become a public charge." Between 1895 and 1915, this provision was responsible for approximately two-thirds of all immigration exclusions.

The "likely public charge" provision was gender-neutral, but it was particularly problematic for single women, especially those who belonged to certain ethnic groups, such as Jewish women.

The difficulties facing single, female immigrants were then further compounded by the 1907 Immigration Act, which prohibited the entry of prostitutes and other women entering for "immoral purposes." After the enactment of this provision, single women attempting to immigrate alone ran a high risk of being accused of prostitution or other immorality. The experience of Martha Ash, a young New Zealander, is illustrative. In 1918, Ash left New Zealand to join her fiancé in America. Upon arrival, some of Ash's fellow passengers claimed she had behaved improperly with one of the officers. As a result, she was deemed a woman entering for "immoral purposes" and denied entry. Ash vehemently denied the accusations, but her word was insufficient to overcome the charges. In the end, it was only her fiancé's continued willingness to marry her that prevented Ash's deportation.

America's xenophobic immigration restrictions were designed to keep out a broad category of "undesirable" immigrants, and this goal was furthered by the racist pseudoscience of the early-twentieth-century eugenics movement. Eugenicists advocated for stronger immigration restrictions by claiming that traits such as criminality and immorality were hereditary and more likely to exist in certain immigrant populations. They also warned that "undesirable" immigrants were reproducing at a faster rate than America's white middle and upper classes and without restrictions would soon outnumber them. In 1906, President Theodore Roosevelt echoed these eugenic fears when he famously described declining white birth rates as "race suicide" and a problem "infinitely more important than any other question in this country."

US anti-venereal-disease poster from World War I, 1918.

As America entered World War I, these fears continued to intensify. During the war, military propaganda portrayed foreign women as either dangerous spies or diseased harlots. Congress then compounded these fears when it expanded the enemy alien statute to permit the arrest and confinement of foreign-born wives suspected of aiding the enemy. Consequently, when American soldiers started bringing home foreign brides, many Americans worried these were the sort of dangerous or debauched women they had been taught to fear. Social workers helping to process war brides also fueled these perceptions. Maude Cleveland, head of the war brides division of the Red Cross, was appalled that many of the women readily admitted to marrying for immigration benefits, and she implored the

American public to "wake up" and recognize that foreign brides were "preying upon the American army."

Americans like Cleveland condemned women who had married for immigration benefits while ignoring the compelling circumstances that often motivated their marital decisions. Europe had been decimated by World War I, and many war brides had suffered terribly. Some were widows with young children, others were survivors of disease and starvation, and nearly all had seen the places they lived and people they loved destroyed by conflict. Immigration offered these women the opportunity to rebuild their lives, but as single immigrants, many would have been denied entry as too poor, too sick, or too "immoral." For these women, marriage was their only immigration option, and as immigration restrictions continued increasing after the war, more and more women made this marital choice.

In 1917, Congress enacted a literacy requirement and barred entry to immigrants who could not read. Then, in 1921, it passed the Emergency Quota Act, which established numerical limits on the number of immigrants who could enter the US and specifically limited immigration from certain "undesirable" countries — primarily Eastern and Southern Europe. Both restrictions made entry drastically harder for millions of potential immigrants. In 1921, a *Harper's Magazine* article recounted the immigration hearing of a thirty-seven-year-old Greek seamstress ensnared by the literacy requirement. In the article, the woman is described as "attractive and well dressed and obviously makes a good impression on the [immigration] board. But unfortunately, she is illiterate." When she is handed a book, she mutters the word "upsilon" because, as the article notes, "It is evidently the only letter she can recognize." The woman was a refugee whose family "had all been killed by the Turks," but this tragedy was irrelevant to her immigration petition. Marriage, however, would have provided an exception. As the article noted, "If she

THE AMERICANESE WALL, AS CONGRESSMAN BURNETT WOULD BUILD IT.
UNCLE SAM: You're welcome in — if you can climb it!

The American wall, as Congressman Burnett would build it. Uncle Sam: You're welcome in — if you can read it!

had been married, and were coming to join her husband . . . the literacy provision of the law would not have kept her out." Unfortunately, she was single, so she was deported.

For many would-be immigrants, marriage was their only immigration option and, frequently, their only path to safety. Such motivations are poignantly apparent in the immigration interview of a young Armenian woman also attempting to enter the United States in 1921. The woman was a mail-order bride, and when immigration officials asked her why she agreed to marry a man she had never met she replied bluntly, "It is better to marry a stranger than to be massacred." Marriage was the sole

W. H. Auden and Erika Mann pictured in the year of
their marriage by Alec Bangham, 1935.

way this woman, a near victim of the Armenian genocide, could
find safety in America. Her story was not unique.

In the 1930s, as the Nazi threat increased throughout Europe,
America and other Western countries continued to restrict
immigration. As a result, marital immigration literally became
a lifesaving strategy. In one famous example, the poet W. H.
Auden, who was homosexual, married Erika Mann, author
Thomas Mann's daughter, to help her escape the Nazis. The
following year, Auden persuaded the novelist John Hampson to
marry a friend of Erika's, the actress Therese Giehse, who was
also under threat for her anti-Nazi activities. When a friend tried
to dissuade Hampson from the marriage, he refused and replied,
"Wystan [his name for Auden] says, 'What are buggers for?'"

Marital immigration saved women's lives, but it could also
encourage their exploitation. World War II was devastat-
ing even for those who had not faced direct persecution, and

American troops entering Naples, 1943.

when the war ended, countless men and women were eager
to leave their war-torn countries. For many desperate female
immigrants, marriage was their best, or only, chance to escape.
Sadly, American soldiers were not above exploiting this situation. Anna Della Casa, a sixteen-year-old Neapolitan teenager,
was faced with this difficult choice when, at the war's conclusion, she received a marriage proposal from a thirty-five-year-
old American soldier. Anna came from a family of eighteen, all
of whom were struggling to survive. On October 1, 1943, when
the Allied troops entered Naples, the local population had no
food, water, or electricity. The Della Casas also had no home.
The retreating Germans had burned down the family's home,
and Anna, her parents, and her siblings were all squeezed into
a married sister's small apartment. At the strong urging of her
parents, Anna agreed to marry her American suitor. This ensured
her parents had one less mouth to feed, and it guaranteed Anna's
entry into America. However, it was not a love match. Years
later, when asked why she married, Anna touched a shrapnel

scar on her neck and answered, "To get me out of the nightmare of the war. I dreamed of the bombs, the bombs, the bombs."

Similar desperation is apparent in the 1953 immigration fraud case *U.S. v. Lutwak*. Shortly after World War II ended, Marcel Lutwak and his mother attempted to bring their relatives, survivors of the Nazi concentration camps, into the United States. Lutwak, Bessie Osborne, and Grace Klemtner, all military veterans, agreed to take advantage of the spousal immigration benefit accorded discharged veterans. The three agreed they would "pretend" to marry Maria, Munio, and Leopold Knoll, in order to bring them to the United States. Speed was particularly important for Munio, who had been starved and beaten in the camps and needed urgent medical care. The couples married in Paris and then immigrated to America, but they never lived together. Eventually, their scheme was discovered, and they were convicted of immigration fraud. Years later, Lutwak was pardoned by President Nixon in a belated recognition of the justness of his marital decision.

Marrying for Government Benefits Today: Perpetuating Inequality

Nearly two hundred years after the first Widows' Pension Act was passed, the practice of attaching federal benefits to marriage continues. This link encourages couples, and especially women, to marry, but such marriages remain problematic. Marrying for government benefits is primarily a strategy of the desperate, and limiting benefits to the married excludes other needy and deserving individuals. Even more concerningly, this link between marriage and government benefits continues to perpetuate gender and racial inequality. Marital immigration remains one obvious example of this problem.

Marrying for Immigration Benefits

Today, marrying for a green card (entry into the United States) remains perfectly legal. A marital immigrant does not need to be in love. The only requirement is they intend to make a life with their American spouse. This is known as the "establish a life test." In the 1996 case *U.S. v. Tagalicud*, the Ninth Circuit Court of Appeals affirmed the legality of such marriages while also, inadvertently, highlighting the reason why they are worrying. In describing the difference between marital immigration and marital fraud, the court explained that marrying for a visa does not, by itself, constitute fraud, because the immigrant spouse could have "intended to establish a life together at the time they were married in gratitude for the visa."

Historically, the circumstances that inspired the type of gratitude described by the *Tagalicud* court included genocide, persecution, and starvation, and many modern marital immigrants are responding to similar conditions. One recent, non-American, example involves Syrian women marrying to escape German refugee camps. As refugees, these women were subject to movement and travel bans that effectively imprisoned them in these camps. Desperate to escape these camps, many began asking relatives to find them German Syrian men willing to marry them so they could finally leave the camps. These women might have the type of "gratitude" toward their husbands that the *Tagalicud* court was envisioning.

When marriage is the only option for victims of war, persecution, and genocide, it can increase the vulnerability of already vulnerable people. In the United States, marital immigrants are dangerously dependent on their citizen spouse. After the American citizen (or lawful permanent resident) petitions for their spouse's admission to the US, the immigrant spouse remains dependent on the citizen for this immigration benefit and needs their ongoing cooperation to gain permanent legal status. If an immigrant spouse is divorced or abandoned by their American spouse before gaining their own, independent, immigration status, they can be deported, and this dependency can increase the likelihood the immigrant spouse may be abused.

The link between marriage and immigration can also lead to abuse of the citizen sponsor. Marital immigration remains one of the quickest, if not only, options for many would-be immigrants. As a result, underage, American girls are sometimes forced to marry foreign men to facilitate their immigration into the US. Naila Amin was fifteen when her family ordered her to marry a twenty-eight-year-old man and bring him into the United States. Amin blames her family for forcing her into an abusive marriage but also recognizes the marriage would not have happened absent US immigration law's marital preference. As Amin notes, "People die to come to America. I was a passport to him. They all wanted him here, and that was the way to do it."

Linking marriage to immigration can incentivize abuse. However, the problem with connecting federal benefits to marriage is not limited to immigration. In fact, marriage-based monetary benefits may be even more concerning.

Marriage and Government Money

Beginning in the 1930s, the number of women eligible for marriage-based federal support increased significantly, but this change was not made for their benefit. Rather, it was to counteract women's growing employment opportunities and encourage them to remain in the home and financially dependent on their

Unemployed, single women protesting the job placement of married women before themselves at the Emergency Relief Administration headquarters in Boston, Massachusetts.

husbands. By linking financial benefits to marriage, the government could argue that women didn't need formal economic equality with men, such as equal work or wages, because they would receive their economic protections through marriage. As historian Nancy Cott explains, great effort was taken to ensure "that the 'working girl' was the only approved female wage earner — someone passing through a phase of her life, for whom paid work was fleeting and not a continuing need and right, who could manage without equal work and did not merit the same say in government or union policy as the 'working man.'" Female employment was envisioned as temporary support for unmarried women; marriage was how women were really expected to "earn" their money. Many New Deal programs reflected this conception of female work, but the Social Security Act of 1935 (SSA) was one of the clearest.

A monthly check to you for the rest of your life, beginning when you are 65, 1935.

The SSA was promoted as an earned entitlement — not public assistance. Recipients were envisioned as able-bodied, mostly white, male workers who were insuring themselves against future circumstances. Women were not part of this vision, as Congress made abundantly clear when it chose the SSA over a far more evenhanded bill also pending before Congress. This alternative legislation, the Workers Unemployment and Social Insurance Act, would have provided old-age, unemployment, and health benefits for all wage workers regardless of age, race,

Why the Workers' Unemployment Insurance Bill? How
It Can Be Won, 1933.

sex, origin, or politics. Instead, Congress enacted the SSA.
This act excluded most women, as well as a large percentage of
non-white workers, through the provisions omitting part-time,
seasonal, agricultural, domestic, philanthropic, and government
employees including teachers and self-employed workers — the
jobs typically held by women and people of color.

Four years after passing the SSA, Congress amended the
act to provide for women, but in their role as wives rather than
workers. Under the amendments, women were eligible for
Social Security benefits based on their husbands' earnings and
would receive support when their breadwinning husband died

or retired. The act also incentivized men to marry by ensuring they would receive 50 percent more Social Security income at retirement (through Social Security payments to the man's wife) than they would receive if they remained single.

The SSA amendments were modeled on the traditional marital bargain. Men received a government pension for working, while women received a pension for marrying a man who worked. If a woman's husband died before her children were grown, the government would assume his role and provide cash assistance. If she was widowed later in life, she would receive a portion of her husband's Social Security benefits. Today, the implications of the government's decision to support women through marriage, not employment, remain substantial.

Nearly a hundred years after the SSA was enacted, women still have worse employment prospects than men and are significantly more likely to be poor. The average woman earns only 83 cents for every dollar earned by a man. She also earns approximately $10,000 less per year than her male counterpart and $500,000 less over the course of her working life. Lower wages also mean the average female worker receives a substantially smaller Social Security check. In 2017, the average monthly Social Security benefit of a retired man was $1,503, while the average monthly benefit of a retired woman was $1,196. This inequality is known as the gender wage gap.

The SSA addresses this wage gap by permitting a low- or non-earning wife to receive Social Security benefits based off her husband's higher salary. However, this solution does nothing to remedy the underlying problem of female wage and employment discrimination. Rather, by obscuring the true extent of female employment discrimination, the SSA helps perpetuate it. In 2019, 43 percent of women received Social Security benefits based on their husband's earnings. In 2095, it is estimated that 25 percent of women will still rely on their husband's earnings in their Social Security benefits calculations. That means, for the next seventy-five years, at least one-quarter of American women are expected to have fewer job opportunities and receive lower wages than their male peers and to rely on marriage for their long-term financial security.

Marriage and Tax Benefits

By linking government support with marriage, the SSA encourages female economic dependency. The federal tax code is similar. Like the SSA, the tax code rewards couples willing to assume the traditional marital roles of male wage earner and female dependent. When a high earner marries a lower- or non-earning spouse, marriage significantly reduces their average tax rate. This can mean thousands of dollars in tax savings. In fact, the marriage tax "bonus" can be as high as 21 percent of the couple's total income. However, not all married couples receive tax benefits. Similar-earning spouses can face a marriage penalty, meaning they pay more taxes as a couple than they did as individuals.

The tax code turns women's typically lower earnings into a benefit and can disincentivize female employment entirely. Because most married couples will file jointly, their income gets lumped together on their return. This can pull the higher earner's income into a lower tax rate. But this lumping together may also mean that the lower-earning spouse's income is taxed at a higher rate than it was when she was unmarried. Consequently, after marriage, and especially after the birth of children, it may no longer be financially beneficial for the lower-earning partner

"'Single'? With *this* kind of income?
Oh, have I got a dependent for *you!*"

Tax examiner cartoons and comics.

to work. A relatively low-earning spouse, typically the wife, may be taxed at such a high rate after marriage that the amount she receives after taxes doesn't come close to covering childcare. In such instances, wives would literally be paying to work. As a result, many women make the financially reasonable decision to quit the workforce and rely entirely on their husband's earnings.

The Marriage Cure

Both the tax code and the SSA treat marriage as a solution to female financial inequality and as a cure for female poverty. Scholars have dubbed this solution the marriage cure. For the

Pro-marriage billboard

past thirty years, it has been a major part of US welfare policy. In 1996, Congress passed the Personal Responsibility Work Opportunity Reconciliation Act (PRWORA). The act cited declining marriage rates as the primary cause of child poverty and intergenerational poverty and authorized states to use federal and state Temporary Assistance to Needy Families (TANF) funds to encourage welfare recipients to marry. Initially, these funds were used for pro-marriage expenditures such as billboards, handbooks, marital education programs, and relationship skills classes. Then, over the following decade, the money spent on pro-marriage, anti-poverty efforts increased. In 2000, the US Department of Health and Human Services authorized $10 million to be used to reward states with the greatest growth in the proportion of children living in homes headed by a married couple. In 2002 and 2003, it allocated $90 million to marriage-related research and demonstration projects, and in 2006, Congress reauthorized PRWORA and appropriated an annual $150 million in federal money (for five years) for state marriage promotion efforts.

During this period, states also funded marriage promotion efforts, and some even paid poor people to marry. Under Wisconsin's marriage promotion or "bridefare" program, couples

Marriage and relationship tip billboard.

on welfare received an extra $80 per month if they married, and in West Virginia, they received an extra $100. Similarly, under Minnesota's program, married parents were allowed to exclude more income from their welfare benefit calculations than unmarried parents, which increased the size of their welfare payments. These financial incentives convinced some couples to marry, but they were not the poverty solution Congress had envisioned. Poor husbands can't solve female poverty. As law professor Angela Onwuachi-Willig notes, "At a most basic level, if Congress wants to institute a marriage cure to poverty, it must support such efforts by creating jobs for the potential future spouses of women welfare recipients." Until Congress makes these changes, encouraging poor women to marry will do more harm than good.

In her 2012 book, *The End of Men*, journalist Hannah Rosin highlights this problem when she describes a grocery store encounter with a young woman named Bethanny. Bethanny was a single mother running an in-home day care and studying to become a nurse. Rosin describes her as a woman in a precarious financial position, forced to haggle over supermarket coupons and snacks but intent on financial improvement. Bethanny is economically better off than the women in the bridefare programs, but not by much. If marriage were an obvious financial benefit, it is likely she would have married. However, her conversation with Rosin underscores the danger of encouraging low-income women like Bethanny to wed their most likely marriage prospects — similarly low-income men.

The father of Bethanny's child was a man named Calvin. Calvin was a sporadically employed house painter who rarely contributed money to Bethanny or their daughter. When Rosin asked Bethanny why she didn't marry Calvin, both she and her daughter laughed. Bethanny then pointed to her shopping cart and explained that marrying Calvin would mean "one fewer granola bar for us." Bethanny believed that without good job prospects and a stable income, marrying Calvin was financially harmful, and she was probably correct.

In modern America, individual financial security is largely based on a person's "employability." Marriage to a person with the education, skills, and experience to succeed in a competitive labor pool can be beneficial, but when one or both of the parties lack employability, like a large majority of welfare recipients, marriage is unlikely to provide security and stability. Poor women tend to have lower levels of education and work experience than richer women and, if they marry at all, are likely to marry men who are also low-wage earners. As family law professors Naomi Cahn and June Carbone have explained, "Practically, this means that while marriage is a source of strength for couples who can trade off childcare and workforce participation in ways that allow the family to marshal the resources necessary for investment in children and in adult 'employability,' it can be a threat to working class families." Although the government has long assumed marriage reduces poverty, there is little support for this conclusion.

Today, one of the most comprehensive marriage promotion programs created under PRWORA, the Supporting Healthy

Marriage project, is widely regarded as a failure. The program was a rigorous multiyear, multisite program that provided marriage education to low-income married couples. It included six thousand couples, provided four to five months of classes and programs per couple, and cost more than $50 million or approximately $9,100 per couple. However, despite the generous funding and the dozens of hours of programs and services each participating couple received, the treatment and control groups had the same likelihood of divorce. The program was a fiasco, and even the study's authors concluded that it would be "worthwhile [to consider] whether this amount of money could be spent in ways that bring about more substantial effects on children and families." Such advice has largely gone unheeded; promoting marriage as a poverty cure remains politically popular. In 2016, then presidential candidate Jeb Bush described marriage as "the most effective anti-poverty program." In 2017, Florida senator Marco Rubio declared marriage "the greatest tool to lift children and families from poverty," and most recently, in 2021, Missouri senator Josh Hawley released his "pro family and pro work" plan, which sought to encourage marriage, and thus reduce poverty, by giving married couples double the child tax credit available to single parents.

Government benefits can incentivize women, particularly poor women, to marry, but most would profit more from policies that directly address the causes of poverty — the lack of livable wages, family leave, and health care — than those promoting marriage. Moreover, as history demonstrates, linking vital government benefits to marriage can encourage harmful and exploitive marriages while reducing the government's interest in finding more effective solutions to the economic, gender, and racial inequality perpetuating these problems. Finally, conditioning government benefits on marriage is also problematic, because it encourages couples to marry for reasons other than love. If love is the purpose of marriage, then attaching government benefits impedes this goal. Common sense dictates that the more benefits are combined with marriage, the more people will marry for these advantages. If Americans truly believe people should marry for love, then the government should stop giving them so many non-love reasons to marry.

chapter three

The Power Couple:
Marrying for Status and Power

The only thing worse than smug married couples: lots of smug married couples.

— BRIDGET JONES

In the novel *Bridget Jones's Diary*, the protagonist, a single, thirty-something Londoner, refers to her coupled friends as "smug marrieds." Jones uses the term to indicate the higher status that married couples enjoy, and although she rejects the idea that "marrieds" are better than "singletons" (her name for single people), she acknowledges the very real connection between marriage and status. Despite her outward disdain for the smug marrieds, Bridget Jones wants nothing more than to join their ranks.

After publication of *Bridget Jones's Diary*, the word *singleton* quickly became part of modern English vernacular. When author Helen Fielding was asked about the term's origin, she explained, "A friend made it up for a party: singletons in one hotel, marrieds in another!" She then noted that the reason she liked it so much, and included it in her novels, was that it was a positive substitute for *spinster*. Fielding described *spinster* — the long-standing term for an unmarried woman — as "horrible," because of its "connotations of spinning wheels failure." *Singleton*, she suggested, is a much more positive word and has the added benefit of "appl[ying] to both men and women."

Spinsters and Bachelors in Colonial America

Fielding is far from the first to note the deep-seated connection between non-marriage and failure. For centuries, marriage has been a marker of status. Married people were treated with dignity and admiration, while the unmarried were relegated to the social bottom. This disdain applied to both men and women, but the reasons were different.

In colonial America, unmarried women were seen as failures. As marriage historian Elizabeth Abbott notes, "The spinster was never to forget — nor to be forgiven for — the fact that she was not a wife." Rebecca Dickinson, an unmarried woman living in Hatfield, Massachusetts, during the late eighteenth century, was frequently the target of such scorn and detailed it in her private journals. In one entry from 1787, Dickinson writes, "How often have they hissed and wagged their heads at me by reason of my solitary life." In another entry, she recounts a mortifying conversation with "[a] woman who had been exceedingly prosperous in the world [who] asked me whether I was not Sorry that I Did not marry when I was young." Dickinson was "thunderstruck" by the question. She was a skilled and financially successful dressmaker, and she angrily responded, "My affairs might be in a worse situation." Still, despite this outward bravado, the incident left her heartbroken and feeling "more than ever" like a "poor bird that was picked of all its feathers." Dickinson writes that after the encounter she "cried all the day without cessation." However, her distress was more than just a reaction to the woman's rudeness. Dickinson feared such criticisms were justified, that "to see an old maid after fifty is a Sight that would make any woman wonder." Dickinson never forgot the encounter: "It [was] one of my youthful Days Carryed into old age."

The scorn faced by women like Dickinson was heartrending, but it paled in comparison with the loathing directed at single

men. Free of the legal obligations of marriage, colonial communities believed bachelors would seduce single women and then abandon them and their children to become financial burdens on the public. Marriage was what transformed these potentially irresponsible men into dependable husbands and fathers, and those who refused to marry were treated as threats and undeserving of the label "man."

George Washington expressed this view of the unmarried when he advised his nephew to marry so he could "quit the trifling amusements of a boy and assume the more dignified manners of a man." Benjamin Franklin voiced similar sentiments when he variously described bachelors as "not yet a complete man" but only "half a man," as "one half of a pair of scissors," and as having "not nearly the value he would have in a state of union." Franklin's contempt for bachelors is also apparent in his story "The Speech of Polly Baker," in which he highlights the unfairness of charging women for having children out of wedlock but not prosecuting the fathers. In the story, Polly acknowledges that she is an unmarried mother but claims the real criminal is the bachelor who promised to marry her and then abandoned her and their child. She tells her accusers, "Take into your wise consideration, the great and growing number of bachelors in the country, many of whom, from the mean fear of the expenses of a family, have never sincerely and honorably courted a woman in their lives; and by their manner of living leave unproduced (which is little better than murder) hundreds of their posterity to the thousandth generation. Is not this a greater offense against the public good than mine?"

John and Abigail Adams also viewed bachelors with deep disdain. In a 1777 letter to John, Abigail recounts a vicious attack on a merchant whom she pointedly refers to as "a bachelor." The man was accused of hoarding sugar and coffee (commodities she notes "the female part of this state is very loath to give up"), and as a result, he was attacked by an enraged female mob. According to Abigail, the women violently seized the man, "tossed him into the cart," and distributed his goods. Meanwhile, the town's men "stood amazed, silent spectators of the whole transaction." John's lighthearted response to this violence was "the women in Boston begin to think themselves able to serve their country." Neither John nor Abigail expressed any sympathy for the bachelor who had been beaten and robbed. According to Professor Mark Kann, "The remarkable thing about this exchange is that both Adamses were consistently horrified by mob actions, but responded here with humor, apparently because the 'victim' was a bachelor who stood beneath men's contempt and, importantly, beyond protection of law."

In colonial America, marriage was what transformed irresponsible and potentially dangerous males into trustworthy members of society. It is also what qualified them for political rights. In a 1776 letter to Virginia politician Edmund Pendelton, Thomas Jefferson notes this connection between marriage and political rights, writing, "I cannot doubt any attachment to his country in any man who has his family . . . in it . . . I am for extending the right of suffrage (or in other words the rights of a citizen) to all who [have] a permanent intention of living in the country. Take what circumstances you please as evidence of this, either having resided a certain time, or having a family or having property any or all of them."

At the constitutional convention, George Mason also noted the connection between marriage and political rights when he argued that voting should not be limited to landholders. He stated:

> A freehold is the qualification in England and hence it is imagined to be the only proper one. The true idea [is] that every man having evidence of attachment to and permanent common interest with the society ought to share in its rights and privileges. Was this qualification restrained to freeholders? Does no other kind of property but land evidence a common interest in the proprietor? Does nothing besides property make a permanent attachment? Ought . . . the parent of a number of children whose fortunes are to be pursued in his own country to be viewed as suspicious characters and unworthy to be trusted with the common rights of their fellow citizens?

Alexander Hamilton took these ideas even further when he suggested that marriage and fatherhood were crucial qualifications for political leadership because such men were the least likely to abuse political power. A father, explained Hamilton, would not choose "the precarious enjoyment of rank and power" or participate in a "system which would reduce his posterity . . . to slavery and ruin." Instead, he would approach the future with caution and his children would serve as "the dearest pledges of [his] patriotism." Hamilton argued that marriage made men trustworthy, and that citizens would have the greatest confidence in a leader who was "the father of children to whom the ties of nature and habit have attached."

Marriage as Political Alliance

Marriage demonstrated suitability for political rights and power, but it could also confer power more directly. Politically strategic marriages were not uncommon in colonial America, and one of the most famous examples is that of Alexander Hamilton and Elizabeth Schuyler. Thanks to Lin-Manuel Miranda's musical *Hamilton*, the story of Hamilton marrying for political advantage is well known. In one song, Angelica Schuyler sings about this marital motivation:

> *He's after me because I'm a Schuyler sister*
> *That elevates his status*
> *I'd have to be naive to set that aside*
> *Maybe that is why I introduce him to Eliza*
> *Now that's his bride*

Marriage gave Hamilton access to the powerful Schuyler family, and this alliance helped him become one of the most politically influential men of his era. However, although the Hamilton-Schuyler marriage is one of the most famous, some of the most common political marriages of the eighteenth century were those between white fur traders and Native

Family members of Jean-Baptiste and Pelagie Faribault, circa 1850. Pictured are their son Alexander (standing at left); their grandson George (seated at left); and George's bride, Euphrasine St. Antoine (seated at center). Jean-Baptiste is seated on the far right. Father Augustin Ravoux stands between Jean-Baptiste and Euphrasine.

women. As historian Catherine Denial writes, "A central skill of any successful fur trader was an eye for opportunity, especially when it came to judging which alliances would generate the most financial and political gain." White fur traders were eager to marry into politically powerful Native families, while many Native women were equally interested in the political and economic benefits of having an American husband. The marriage of Jean-Baptiste Faribault, a white trader, with Elizabeth Pelagie Ainse, a Dakota woman, is illustrative of such a politically advantageous marriage.

Jean-Baptiste and Pelagie were married in 1805 when the Dakota were a powerful tribe occupying large areas of Minnesota and Wisconsin. Through marriage, Jean-Baptiste

View of Wita Tanka (Pike's Island) and Fort Snelling from Mendota. Painting by Edward Kirkbride Thomas, circa 1850.

gained access to the tribe's valuable hunting lands and a close connection to the tribe. Pelagie, in turn, gained access to the territory's increasingly important white community. In 1819, these connections became especially valuable when Colonel Henry Leavenworth arrived in the Minnesota territory seeking land for the construction of a new fort needed to halt Britain's westward expansion and disrupt its long dominance of the fur trade. Leavenworth quickly identified a desirable location for the intended fort. However, the land was part of the Dakota Territory, and Leavenworth needed help negotiating with the tribe. He sought the assistance from the Faribaults, who then successfully negotiated a fifteen-acre parcel of land for the desired fort. In return for this aid, the couple received a parcel of property known as Pike's Island. Then, seventeen years after the Faribaults were gifted Pike's Island, the US attempted to take it back.

The government claimed the 1837 Treaty of St. Peters, which negotiated the cession of land in Wisconsin and Minnesota, included Pike's Island. The Faribaults vehemently disagreed, and when they learned of the government's plan to steal their land, they quickly took action. They contacted their friend Samuel Stambaugh, the Indian agent out of Green Bay (who had helped negotiate the 1837 treaty), and had him advise the government that it would be wise to back off. In a letter to J. R. Poinsett, the US secretary of war, Stambaugh warned that "the Faribault family is the most powerful and influential among the Sioux Indians" and that angering them could have dire consequences. He further noted, "It is families of this description who do much good or much evil among the Indians with whom they are connected by bonds of blood; and [the] government would save much blood and treasure, if proper pains were taken to secure their friendship." Poinsett got the message. Instead of taking the Faribaults' land, the government paid for it. Through marriage, a frontier fur trader and his Dakota wife had become powerful enough to intimidate the US government.

The Political Influence of Wives

Pike's Island had been gifted to Pelagie in her own name, in accordance with Dakota custom and tradition. As a Dakota woman, Pelagie possessed political rights separate from her husband and her marriage. Pelagie's white contemporaries rarely had such power. In early America, women's political influence was grounded in marriage. This was a significant limitation. Still, the power women wielded as wives could be substantial. In fact, many of the founders, including John Adams, believed that while men cast the votes, it was their wives who determined for what and for whom they voted. Adams even predicted it would be married women, not men, who ultimately decide whether a "Republican government is practicable in a nation or not."

Portrait of a young Abigail Adams by Benjamin Blyth, painted in 1766.

John's wife, Abigail, agreed with her husband that women's political influence derived from marriage. However, she was significantly less sanguine about this fact. Abigail feared that marriage-based political rights were too precarious and that many husbands would ignore their wives' concerns and interests. In her famous letter to John regarding the rights of women, she suggested that women should be granted rights as individuals and not forced to rely on marriage:

> In the new code of laws which I suppose it will be necessary for you to make, I desire you would remem-

ber the ladies and be more generous and favorable to them than your ancestors. Do not put such unlimited power into the hands of the husbands. Remember, all men would be tyrants if they could. If particular care and attention is not paid to the ladies, we are determined to foment a rebellion, and will not hold ourselves bound by any laws in which we have no voice or representation . . . That your Sex are Naturally Tyrannical is a Truth so thoroughly established as to admit of no dispute, but such of you as wish to be happy willingly give up the harsh title of Master for the more tender and endearing one of Friend. Why then, not put it out of the power of the vicious and the Lawless to use us with cruelty and indignity with impunity. Men of Sense in all Ages abhor those customs which treat us only as the vassals of your Sex. Regard us then as Beings placed by providence under your protection and in imitation of the Supreme Being make use of that power only for our happiness.

Adams ignored his wife's suggestion and, in doing so, proved her point.

Marriage was a risky basis upon which to ground women's political rights. Still, the power women gained through marriage could be significant. In the 1830s, Alexis de Tocqueville traveled the United States and recorded his impressions of the American democratic experiment — including the role of women. De Tocqueville noted that American women forfeited many legal rights by choosing to marry but concluded that marriage remained to their advantage. "I do not hesitate to avow that although the women of the United States are confined within the narrow circle of domestic life, and their situation is in some respects one of extreme dependence . . . I have nowhere seen woman occupying a loftier position." De Tocqueville even suggested it was because of the limitations imposed by marriage that American women wielded such power and influence. He wrote:

> The Americans do not think that man and woman have either the duty or the right to perform the same offices, but they show an equal regard for both their respective parts; and though their lot is different, they consider both of them as beings of equal value. They do not give to the courage of woman the same form or the same direction as to that of man, but they never doubt her courage; and if they hold that man and his partner ought not always to exercise their intellect and understanding in the same manner, they at least believe the understanding of the one to be as sound as that of the other, and her intellect to be as clear. Thus, then, while they have allowed the social inferiority of woman to continue, they have done all they could to raise her morally and intellectually to the level of man; and in this respect they appear to me to have excellently understood the true principle of democratic improvement.

De Tocqueville also credited American wives as the reason for America's unexpected success. "If I were asked, now that I am drawing to the close of this work, in which I have spoken of so many important things done by the Americans, to what the singular prosperity and growing strength of that people ought mainly to be attributed, I should reply: To the superiority of their women."

Marriage as a Race Changer

Marriage helped women regain some of the status and power denied due to their sex, and in the pre–Civil War period, some African Americans used marriage in a similar manner. During the colonial period, free persons of color who possessed less than a specified degree of black blood, usually a quarter or eighth, were designated "white" and entitled to legal and social privileges that came with that status. As a result, intermarriage offered black men and women a way to secure preferential racial status for their descendants. This was one reason why colonial whites viewed intermarriage as so threatening.

In 1757, the Virginia reverend Peter Fontaine wrote to his brother in Wales lamenting the practice of intermarriage, stating, "This abominable practice . . . hath polluted the blood of many amongst us." Fontaine was particularly distraught by the fact that under the law, children of mixed-race families could eventually become white. As Fontaine noted, descendants "but three generations removed from the black father or mother, may, by the indulgence of the laws of the country, intermarry with the white people, and actually do every day so marry."

State anti-miscegenation laws were enacted to prevent interracial marriages and the "dangers" Fontaine noted, but these laws could be flouted. In 1819 a Scotsman named James Flint traveled to America and spent eighteen months in the town of Jeffersonville, Indiana. Shortly after arriving in Indiana, Flint wrote a letter describing how a "negro man and a white woman came before the squire of a neighbouring township, for the purpose of being married." Initially, the official refused to conduct the wedding service, citing the state's prohibition on "all sexual intercourse between white and coloured people." Then, a short time later, he changed his mind. The official "suggested, that if the woman could be qualified to swear that there was black blood in her, the law would not apply." According to Flint, "The hint was taken, and the lancet was immediately applied to the Negro's arm. The loving bride drank the blood, made the necessary oath, and his honour joined their hands, to the great satisfaction of all parties."

Marriages, such as the one Flint described, were one way mixed-race individuals were conceived. Sadly, many others were created from non-consensual sexual relations. Nevertheless, the result of both scenarios was that despite interracial marriage bans, there were many mixed-race individuals in antebellum America who appeared white or at least possibly white. For these children, marriage became an important way of securing the racial privileges they were not legally entitled to possess. The case of Gideon Gibson Jr. is illustrative.

Gideon Gibson Jr.'s father, Gideon Gibson Sr., was a free black man who arrived in the South Carolina backcountry in the 1730s. At the time, South Carolina officials believed he had come to plot a slave revolt, and the governor was so fearful of Gibson Sr.'s intentions that he demanded a personal audience. Gibson Sr. complied with this request but explained to the governor that his sympathies were with white people, not black. To prove this point, Gibson noted he was a landowner, had a white wife, and even owned slaves himself. These facts reassured the governor, who then declared that the Gibsons were "not Negroes nor Slaves but Free people" and granted them hundreds of acres of land to induce them to remain in the state.

Thirty years later, Gibson Sr.'s mixed-race son, Gideon Gibson Jr., was a wealthy landowner and a leader of the South Carolina "regulators" — a group that opposed the taxation and fee system imposed by colonial officials. During one regulator protest, a constable and state militia members were injured, and the Charleston authorities sent Colonel Gabriel Powell to arrest Gibson for his role in the protest. However, upon reach-

Randall L. Gibson, Confederate soldier, US senator from
Louisiana, and great-grandson of Gideon Gibson Jr.

ing Gibson, Powell's men refused to arrest him. Instead, they
abandoned Powell and joined the regulators. Powell was humili-
ated. In retaliation, he sought to have Gibson declared black and
"subject him to the penalties of the negro law." He was unsuccessful. Although the Gideons were descended from a black
man, they had become, legally, white.

In 1783, Charleston merchant and Revolutionary War leader
Henry Laurens cited the Gibson case as proof that intermar-
riage could remove the legal disabilities of race. Laurens wrote,
"Reasoning from the colour carries no conviction. By perseverance

the black may be blanched and the 'stamp of Providence' effec-
tually effaced." Laurens did not actually consider Gibson white.
In fact, he believed mixed-race individuals like Gibson, regardless of their complexion, "ought to continue a separate people."
Nevertheless, he recognized that because Gibson looked white,
was married to a white woman, and was treated as white, he was,
for all intents and purposes, white.

Similar reasoning was used in the 1835 South Carolina Court
of Appeal case *State v. Cantey*, in which the court famously
declared that "a slave cannot be a white man." The *Cantey* court's
statement was not about skin color. Rather, it was a recognition
that classification as white or black depended upon acceptance
within white society. An enslaved person, no matter how light
their skin, was not a member of white society and must be black.
Conversely, a free person accepted by white society must be
white. There were several means of demonstrating white social
acceptance, but as *Cantey* highlighted, marriage was one of the
most effective.

Cantey involved the racial status of three mixed-race men
and, specifically, whether their black ancestry precluded them
from testifying against a white man. The heritage of the men
was not in question. It was accepted that all three descended
from a mixed-race man. Nevertheless, the court held that the
men were white because their ancestor had been treated as
white. As the court explained, the men's "maternal grandfather
. . . although of a dark complexion, had been recognized as a
white man, received into society, and exercised political privileges." Therefore, his descendants were legally white. According
to the court, "For a person of ambiguous appearance, evidence
of reception in society and exercise of legal and political rights
could overcome evidence of negro ancestry." It then cited the
grandfather's marriage with a white woman as conclusive
evidence the man had been accepted as white.

Racial determination cases post-*Cantey* further confirmed that marriage could secure a mixed-race person's designation as white. In an illustrative case from 1840, a Louisiana man named Stephen Boullemet brought a slander suit against an acquaintance for starting a rumor that he was "negro" and imperiling his impending marriage to a white woman. The case turned on whether Boullemet was, in fact, black. To refute this racial allegation, Boullemet presented evidence of acceptance by white society. He called witnesses from the white community of St. Helena, Santo Domingo, where he was raised, to testify that he was "received in good circles of society — He was received as a white man." He also presented specific evidence regarding his mother's race.

During the trial, witnesses testified that after his marriage, Boullemet's father remained an accepted member of Santo Domingo's white society and that such acceptance would not have occurred if Boullemet's mother was black. As one witness explained, "If a white person was to unite to a coloured woman he was immediately considered as degraded." Boullemet argued that because his father remained part of white society after his marriage, his mother must have been white. Boullemet won his case, yet it is highly unlikely his mother was white. In fact, her mixed-race status was so obvious that during the trial, Boullemet was forced to concede she might have been "Indian." Ultimately, his mother's dark complexion and ambiguous racial status didn't matter. By marrying a prominent white husband, she was accepted into white society and became white.

The case of the Wharton family of Stafford County, Virginia, is particularly illustrative of how marriage could change a person's racial status. The Whartons were a formerly enslaved family who had purchased their freedom around 1830. After gaining their freedom, the family chose to remain in Virginia. However, this was forbidden under the state's 1806 removal law requiring all formerly enslaved people freed after May 1, 1806, to leave the commonwealth. Any person who remained in Virginia more than one year after their enslavement ended could be put on trial and, if found guilty, re-enslaved and sold. The 1806 law posed a real threat to the Whartons, but in 1833, fifty-one members of Stafford County's white community submitted a petition to the Virginia legislature arguing that the 1806 law did not apply to the Whartons and that they should be permitted to remain.

Unlike the mixed-race individuals in *Cantey* and *Boullemet*, the Whartons had personally been enslaved and unquestionably met the *Cantey* definition of black. Nevertheless, the Stafford petition asked for a declaration that the Whartons were "white persons" based on the family's appearance and the fact that their most intimate social connections — their marriages — were with white spouses. Shockingly, the legislature granted the request. Despite all evidence to the contrary, it decreed the Whartons were "not negroes or mulattoes, but white persons, although remotely descended from a coloured woman." The Whartons were then permitted to stay.

Intermarriage could help people of color change their racial status, and some individuals, particularly those of mixed racial heritage, explicitly sought out this benefit. In 1821, newspapers in New York, Pennsylvania, and Massachusetts ran the article "A New Chance for Fortune Hunters," which noted the many wealthy, mixed-race Chickasaw women were explicitly looking for white husbands. The article described many of these women as "almost white" and explained they "*prefer white husbands*," because they sought to live as white wives. The article then encouraged white men who had been "unsuccessful speculators in the trade of matrimony" to consider these "handsome women," noting they were "rich in cattle, and horses, and . . . land."

The mixed-race women of the Chickasaw Nation used marriage to secure their desired racial status, and they were far

Abel Stearns and Arcadia Bandini.

from alone. In 1841, Arcadia Bandini married Abel Stearns for similar reasons. Arcadia was the daughter of one of the wealthiest landowning families in the former Mexican territory of California. The family claimed to be white but were most likely of mixed Spanish and indigenous heritage. As a result, their hold on this professed racial designation was tenuous. Arcadia solved this problem by marrying Abel Stearns — a man of indisputable whiteness.

Contemporary accounts describe Stearns as exceedingly ugly. He was severely pockmarked, had a long knife scar running down one cheek, and his long, horse-like face had earned him the nickname Cara de Caballo. He was also nearly thirty years older than Arcadia. However, he was one of the few unquestionably white men in the California Territory. Stearns traced his ancestry back to the Massachusetts Puritans, and this pedigree made him a desirable marriage prospect. By marrying Stearns, Arcadia cemented her racial status and ensured her acceptance into white, Californian society.

One of the most famous examples of marrying for racial status involves the daughters of Richard Johnson, a Kentucky

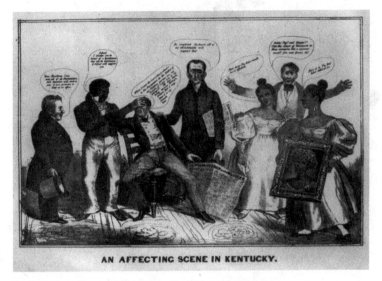

AN AFFECTING SCENE IN KENTUCKY.

Racist political cartoon depicting the Chinn daughters.

congressman and the ninth vice president of the United States (1837–1841). In the early 1800s, Richard Johnson had two daughters, Imogene and Adaline, with an enslaved woman named Julia Chinn. Johnson never freed Julia, but he freed their daughters and sought to have the girls accepted into white society. This goal was highly controversial. In fact, in 1829, the objections to Johnson's relationship with Chinn, whom he publicly referred to as his wife, and his open acknowledgment of his mixed-race daughters was so significant it caused him to lose his Senate seat. Johnson's support of his mixed-race daughters was also used against him during his campaign for the vice presidency. In one particularly racist editorial, penned by partisan journalist Duff Green, Julia Chinn was described as "a jet-black, thick-lipped, odiferous negro wench," and Johnson was condemned for rearing "a family of children whom he endeavored to force upon society as equals." Due to such attacks, Johnson failed to secure enough electoral votes to become vice president, and he is the only vice president in history to be voted into office by the Senate. Despite these political setbacks, Johnson's ultimate goal was achieved. Shortly before becoming vice president, and in exchange for large dowries of valuable farmland, Johnson's mixed-race daughters married well-respected white men. From that moment onward, the Chinn daughters and their descendants were officially regarded as white.

Marriage helped mixed-race individuals secure the legal and social benefits they were denied due to race. In antebellum America, this use of marriage was almost exclusively confined to free persons, but once America entered the Civil War, marriage also helped enslaved individuals gain their freedom. In 1862, Congress passed the Militia Act, which encouraged African American enlistment by guaranteeing freedom to the enlisting soldier as well as "his mother, and his wife and children." In passing this act, Congress recognized that many enslaved men were hesitant to enlist because the wives and children they left behind could be subject to retaliation for the man's desertion. The Militia Act addressed this concern by ensuring enlisting men could take their families with them when they escaped and that these women and children would also be freed.

The connection between marriage and African American freedom continued after the Civil War and became an important part of the debates surrounding the Civil Rights Act of 1866. During these debates, freedom was frequently discussed in relation to marital and familial rights. During one discussion, Senator Jacob Howard of Michigan asked, "What are the attributes of a freeman according to the universal understanding of the American people?" He then answered, "The right of having a family, a wife, children, home." Representative John Kasson of Iowa made a similar point when he declared, "There are three great fundamental natural rights of human society, which you cannot take away without striking a vital blow at the rights of white men as well as black." He listed the rights of a husband to his wife — the marital relation — as the first of these rights. Illinois congressman John Farnsworth echoed these ideas. He asked, "What vested rights [are] so high or so sacred as man's rights to himself, his wife and children, to his liberty and to the fruits of his own industry?"

After the Civil War, many freedmen and -women eagerly embraced marriage and the freedom it represented. Upon receiving the right to marry, one Virginia member of the Colored Infantry proclaimed, "I praise God for this day! I have long been praying for it. The Marriage Covenant is at the foundation of all our rights. In slavery we could not have *legalized* marriage; *now* we have it." A Mississippi chaplain made a similar connection between marriage and freedom when he noted he saw a "very decided improvement in the Social and domestic feelings of those married by the authority and protection of Law. It causes them to feel that they are beginning to be regarded and treated as human beings." Henry Bibb, the famed nineteenth-century author and abolitionist who had been born into slavery, also emphasized the connection between marriage and freedom. He wrote, "There are no class of people in the United States who so highly appreciate the legality of marriage as those persons who have been held and treated as property." To throw off the habits of slavery, Bibbs declared, "regular lawful marriage is a most important thing."

Marriage symbolized black people's free status. As Wake County freedman Parker Pool stated, "Dere wuz no marriage — till after the surrender." At the same time, marriage also came to represent black people's worthiness for freedom. Union officers in command of black troops were some of the first to recognize this role of marriage. As historian Nancy Cott notes in her book *Public Vows*, "Supervisors of black soldiers urged the troops to be 'manly' in marital fidelity as they had been in other ways, to 'set an example for their race,' reminding them that 'the enemies of

"MARRIAGE OF A COLORED SOLDIER AT VICKSBURG BY CHAPLAIN WARREN OF THE FREEDMEN'S BUREAU.

Vicksburg, Mississippi, 1866. This illustration appeared in the June 30, 1866, edition of *Harper's Weekly*. The original drawing was made by the artist Alfred R. Waud (1828–1891).

the colored race who are opposed to their progress and freedom assert that there is no virtue among them.'"

Many newly freed people acted upon such advice and eagerly married. Some even remarried. One newly freed woman explained her decision to remarry her husband of thirty-five years, stating that she was doing it because "all 'spectable folks is to be married, and we's 'spectable." Unfortunately, the connection between marriage and black worth also meant that the failure to marry was increasingly viewed as a threat to racial acceptance. Recognizing this threat, many black leaders devoted significant time and resources to promoting African American marriage and ensuring it conformed with white expectations. One black preacher exemplified this practice when he admonished his congregation, stating, "Look at de white folks. D'ye eber see a white man want to marry a woman when he had a lawful wife a libing? Neber! I neber heard ob sech a thing in all my life. A white man is 'structed; he knows dat's agin de law and de gospil."

As marriage became "proof" of black respectability, this
induced many freedmen and -women to marry, but it also
encouraged the black community to exert pressure on those who
resisted. In 1867, a Freedman's Bureau official described such
tactics, writing:

> The Colored people of this place are trying to make
> their colored bretheren [*sic*] pay some respect to
> themselves and the laws of the country . . . and stop
> the slave style of living to gather [*sic*] without being
> married. A colored man has been promising to marry
> a girl for the last year [and] has been begging with
> her most of the time. They have had four times set
> for marriage, but at each time has put her of[f] with
> some excuse. The colored men of this place appointed
> a committee to wait on him and see if they could not
> influence him to do better.

In remarking on such coercion, law professor Angela Onwuachi-
Willig notes that in the postwar period the "connection between
marriage and racial acceptance was so powerful that even the
'colonized' defended the civilizing tool of marriage."

Marriage and Social Status

The pressure on African American men and women to marry
was intensified by the fact that African American men had few
other means of acquiring status. By the mid-nineteenth century,
white men were increasingly able to avoid the traditional stigma
attached to non-marriage if they were wealthy. In large urban
centers like New York, affluent bachelors were admired and
even courted. Men's clubs and apartment houses sprang up to

cater to these men. These businesses provided unmarried men with the domestic services traditionally performed by a wife but without any of the obligations of marriage. Many residents described this arrangement as paradise. One wealthy bachelor wrote, "Each member is as much at home as if he were in his own castle; the building . . . is kept with the same neatness, exactness, and comfort as a private dwelling. Every member is a master, without any of the cares or troubles of a master."

Wealth could insulate men from the stigma of being unmarried, but for men without money, marriage remained an important status symbol, and this was especially true for African American males. Black men had fewer opportunities to become wealthy and were specifically encouraged, often by the US government, to look to marriage, rather than wealth, as a source of social status. The government hoped that by linking social status to black men's role as husbands and providers it could minimize its own economic responsibility for the newly freed African Americans — especially for black women and children. The lecture series given by General Clinton B. Fisk, head of the Tennessee Freedmen's Bureau, exemplified such governmental efforts. Fisk told his listeners that to "be a man" meant supporting a wife and family and warned that husbands who failed in this regard would lose the love and respect of their wives. "Your wives will not love you if you do not provide bread and clothes for them," he admonished. "They cannot be happy and greet you with a kiss, when you come home, if they are hungry, ragged, and cold." Poor African American men were encouraged to marry for social status, but when wealthy white women did the same, they received a very different reaction.

Until the Civil War, America's wealthy elite had been largely secure in their social superiority. This changed in the postwar period, when a generation of newly rich Americans sought to breach these class barriers. The infamous social battle between

Caroline Astor (left) and Alva Vanderbilt (costumed for one of her masquerade parties).

Mrs. Caroline Astor, a scion of old-money New York, and the newly rich Alva Vanderbilt highlighted this class struggle. It also showed that marriage was how this battle could be won.

In the late nineteenth century, Caroline Astor controlled entry into New York's high society by limiting invitations to her famous balls. Attendees were almost exclusively "Old New York," meaning families whose money was acquired generations earlier by the city's original Dutch and English settlers. "New-money" families, like the Vanderbilts, were not invited to these events. Alva Vanderbilt was unwilling to accept this state of affairs. She was determined to win acceptance into New York society, and she made it her mission to receive an Astor invitation.

Alva's plan began with the construction of a sumptuous mansion on Manhattan's Fifth Avenue. Then, as the home neared completion, Alva planned an extravagant housewarming party to display the new home's wonders. All the prominent

Alva Vanderbilt in costume for one of her fancy dress balls; Vanderbilt Mansion on Fifth Avenue.

men and women of the city were invited, and the New York press predicted the upcoming Vanderbilt ball would be the party of the century. Finally, when anticipation was at its peak, Alva let it slip that Carrie Astor, Caroline Astor's daughter, was not invited. She explained that Mrs. Astor had not "called," meaning she had not recognized Alva socially and therefore, under the social conventions of the period, Alva "couldn't" invite Carrie. Carrie was devasted, and Caroline Astor capitulated. She sent her coachman to the Vanderbilt mansion with her calling card. Alva Vanderbilt responded with an invitation. Through impressive scheming, the Vanderbilt family gained admission into New York's high society. However, Alva didn't want grudging acceptance; she wanted to outrank families like the Astors. So, to beat Caroline Astor, she wed her daughter to a duke.

In 1891, Alva's daughter, Consuelo Vanderbilt, married the Duke of Marlborough and cemented peer marriage as the way for new-money families to bypass the social controls imposed by

Consuelo Vanderbilt on her wedding day.

families like the Astors. For those with millions, peer marriages were easy to arrange. One year after the Marlborough-Vanderbilt wedding, an article in Henry Labouchere's *Truth* magazine noted that "the dream of the New York 'dollar magnates' was to marry English noblemen," and where "one side has to offer a title and the other side money, the dream is easily realized." Rich Americans were wed to European nobility and completely upended the American class structure. As historian Maureen Montgomery writes in her book *Gilded Prostitution*, due to these marriages, it became increasingly common "for some member of [New York's old-moneyed class] to . . . to find some compatriot who is taboo on the other side of the water to be received with open arms in Belgravia and Mayfair."

Between 1870 and 1910, American women accounted for one-tenth of all English peer marriages and one-half of all foreign alliances made by peers. However, as the practice grew, so did the criticisms. In 1902, William T. Stead, a well-known British newspaper editor (and soon-to-be victim of the *Titanic*), criticized aristocratic English husbands for "regard[ing] the American girl as a means of replenishing the exhausted exchequer, a kind of financial resource, like the Income tax." Stead admonished these husbands, but it was the women's actions that truly bothered him. He wrote, "It is not too much to say that where there is no love in the matter, it is only gilded prostitution, infinitely more culpable from the moral point of view than the ordinary vice into which women are often driven by sheer lack of bread." In 1904, the British novelist H. B. Marriott Watson issued a similar rebuke. He described the American women who married for titles as "cold of heart and cool of head" and was appalled that a woman could "allow her personal ambitions to dictate her sexual relations, rather than marrying for love."

American criticisms of these marriages were equally harsh. In 1906, President Theodore Roosevelt wrote, "I thoroly [*sic*] dislike . . . these international marriages . . . which are not . . . even matches of esteem and liking, but which are based upon the sale of the girl for her money and the purchase of the man for his titles." Congress also condemned such unions and even considered passing laws to ban them. Eventually, the dislike of peer marriages became so widespread that heiresses were specifically praised for not marrying aristocrats.

In 1907, the *New York World* published a piece about the marriage of Miss Mills, a Pittsburgh steel heiress, and warmly commended her for picking "a Pittsburgher though she might have had a Duke or even a Prince." In praising her apparent choice of love over money and status, the editors wrote, "She is not marrying young Mr. Phipps for the money that someday he will have. She has plenty already, and more to come than she can ever spend. And she certainly doesn't marry him for social position, because no Mills needs social position from anyone in New York . . . It is just a love match, pure and simple. There is no exchange of wealth for title, no barter of millions for a coronet."

Criticizing women who married for status rather than love was common at the turn of the twentieth century. However, such criticisms implied that most women had a meaningful choice. This was rarely true. Women were expected to marry. Despite the rhetoric about not marrying for status, women's status remained firmly linked to marriage. In her famous novel *The House of Mirth*, Edith Wharton highlights this expectation when the book's protagonist, an upper-class young woman named Lily Bart, complains to a male friend that people are starting to say she should marry. Bart expects sympathy from her friend. Instead he replies, "Well why don't you? . . . Isn't marriage your vocation? Isn't it what you are all brought up for?" As historian Pat Jalland notes, during this period an unmarried woman was still "judged by her contemporaries to be a human failure, condemned to a lonely life of futility, ridicule or humiliation."

The Continuing Political Power of Wives

In the late nineteenth and early twentieth centuries, women's social status remained firmly linked to marriage. Similarly, their political power also remained tied to marriage, and it is no coincidence that opposition to women's suffrage stemmed in part from the fact that the movement sought to base women's political power on their status as individuals rather than as wives. After the Civil War, when the Fourteenth Amendment was being debated in Congress, senators repeatedly dismissed female enfranchisement as unnecessary based on the view that married

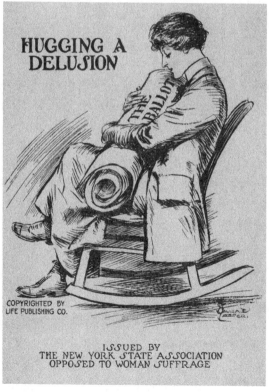

women voted through their husbands. As Senator Timothy
Howe of Wisconsin explained, unlike the freedmen, women
could be denied the vote because "they exercise it by proxy . . .
Females send their votes to the ballot box by their husbands or
other male friends." Senator Ben Wade of Ohio made a similar argument. He described women's suffrage as superfluous
because women were "in high fellowship with those that do
govern," by which he meant they had husbands to "act as their
agents." Others argued against women's suffrage because they
feared giving women the right to vote would detract from their
domestic responsibilities like caring for children and managing
the household.

Maternalist Feminism

Women eventually received the vote, but the difficulties they
encountered convinced many women's rights advocates to focus
on issues that aligned with women's roles as wives and mothers. The maternalist feminism movement arose out of this idea.
Maternalists argued that on certain issues, especially those
relating to child welfare, women were in a superior position to
demand political and social reforms. Maternalists concentrated
on reforms that would improve the lives of women and children, and they were often highly successful. In the early twentieth century, maternalists achieved wage increases and work
hour limits for mothers and children, funded mother's pensions,
passed child labor protections, expanded compulsory education,
and developed juvenile court systems. They also succeeded in
creating the Federal Children's Bureau. Moreover, as law professors Naomi Mezey and Nina Pillard have noted, these achievements were "all the more extraordinary for coming at a time
when women did not have the vote, and when the country

failed to enact social welfare reforms for male industrial workers like those that were emerging in Europe." Maternalism was a successful reform strategy, yet it came at a significant cost.

To achieve their goal, maternalists were willing to limit women's political power and influence to family issues. Historian Lisa D. Brush describes this as "feminism for hard times." By accepting domesticity as the primary source of women's political power, maternalists gained important victories, but they also further entrenched gender inequality and female dependency. During the 1920s and '30s, women's political successes were almost entirely based on their status as wives and mothers.

Given the link between marriage and female political power, it is not surprising that, during this period, the congressional widow emerged as an important political figure. In 1922, shortly after the death of California congressman John Nolan, the California Republican party approached his widow, Mae Ellen Nolan, and encouraged her to run for Nolan's congressional seat. As Nolan's wife, Mae Ellen was assumed to share her husband's political beliefs, thus she was viewed as the ideal replacement. Mae Ellen accepted the nomination, and during her campaign she repeatedly emphasized that as Nolan's wife she was both uniquely qualified and morally obligated to continue his political work. In one speech she declared, "I owe it to the memory of my husband to carry on his work . . . His minimum-wage bill, child labor laws, and national education bills all need to be in the hands of someone who knew him and his plans intimately. No one knows better than I do his legislative agenda." This political strategy was successful and, in a special election held to finish her husband's term and serve the next one, Mae Ellen defeated six opponents and became the fourth woman elected to Congress.

Mae Ellen's political success was not unique. Between 1922 and 1934 eight additional widows were elected to Congress, and it became clear these women had a strong advantage over

Mae Ellen Nolan.

other female candidates. In a study of first-time House candidates elected between 1916 and 1993, 84 percent of widows who ran for office won, while only 14 percent of other non-widowed women were victorious. In fact, of the first one hundred women elected to Congress, more than one-third were widows. In her 1978 study on female political success, political scientist Diane Kincaid quipped that "for women aspiring to serve in Congress, the best husband has been a dead husband, most preferably one serving in Congress at the time of his demise."

The outsized success of congressional widows demonstrated that well into the twentieth century female political power remained most acceptable when it was linked to women's roles as wives and mothers. By claiming the desire to fulfill their husbands' legacies, rather than their own ambitions, these women conformed to accepted gender roles. However, by the mid-twentieth century, this connection between female political power and marriage became increasingly problematic. In 1964, almost two hundred years after John Adams refused his wife's request to "remember the ladies," Congress used nearly identical reasoning to justify its refusal to include women in the Civil

Phyllis Schlafly demonstrating against the Equal Rights Amendment in front of the White House, Washington, DC, February 4, 1977.

Rights Act. The act's opponents reiterated the centuries-old argument that women did not need this political protection because marriage gave them power and influence over their husbands.

During the debate on the women's rights amendment to the Civil Rights Act, Representative Emmanuel Cellar argued against the inclusion of women, stating:

> Mr. Chairman, I heard with a great deal of interest the statement of the gentleman from Virginia that women are in the minority. Not in my house. I can say as a result of 49 years of experience — and I celebrate my 50th wedding anniversary next year — that women, indeed, are not in the minority in my house. As a matter of fact, the reason I would suggest that we have been living in such harmony, such delightful accord for almost half a century is that I usually

have the last two words, and those words are, "Yes,
dear." Of course, we all remember the famous play by
George Bernard Shaw, *Man and Superman*; and man
was not the superman, the other sex was.

Cellar's speech was met with laughter and agreement.

Marriage provided women with a path to political power, yet
it also justified their political exclusion. In the 1970s, the Equal
Rights Amendment (ERA) failed in large part due to maternalist feminists, particularly Phyllis Schlafly. Schlafly claimed that
the family, as "the basic unit of society . . . is the greatest single
achievement in the entire history of women's rights," and that
the special power women wielded within the family would be
lost with the ERA. These arguments proved persuasive, and the
ERA failed.

Marriage and Middle-Class Status

Marriage helped circumvent gender inequality, while simultaneously helping to perpetuate it. The use of marriage to overcome
class barriers produced similarly conflicting results. In 1914, car
manufacturer Henry Ford announced that he was doubling the
minimum rate paid to "[all] married men living with and taking
good care of their families." Until this time, male factory workers had earned too little to support a family on a single wage.
As a result, wage-earning families were largely excluded from
the middle class. Ford's working wage meant married factory
workers could now achieve the middle class "ideal" of a working
husband and a dependent wife.

Support for the working wage quickly expanded. In the 1930s,
social reformers like Katherine Lenroot, chief of the US Children's Bureau, described "a living wage for the father" as "the

primary essential of child welfare." Similarly, US Women's Bureau director Mary Anderson believed the problems of women's wages and working conditions "could be taken care of if the provider for the family got sufficient wages. Then married women would not be obliged to go to work." Such reformers considered working mothers a threat to children's health and development, and for many families the wife's ability to leave the workforce and become a full-time caretaker was beneficial. Nevertheless, as the sole-provider model became more common, this caused problems for women who wished to remain employed.

The rise of the family wage meant women's paid work was increasingly characterized as either temporary (occurring during the expected short period between the end of school and marriage) or unnecessary. Both reasons were then used to justify paying women lower wages. Married women also faced the additional hurdle that their decision to work was considered harmful for their children. Women were expected to put their family first, and working wives, especially working mothers, were viewed as selfish and irresponsible.

Working women were also viewed as a threat to male social status. The family wage made male middle-class status available to wage-earning men, but it was dependent upon husbands fulfilling the breadwinning role. As Professors Marion Crain and Ken Matheny have noted, "The business of making a living was fundamentally a man's business and women were not welcomed because by competing for what were seen as male jobs they threatened men's breadwinner status." Male and female workers became pitted against each other. Wage-earning men, through their unions, responded to the threat of female workers in three stages. First, they supported safety laws limiting the type of work women could do. Later, they used their superior organizational power to maintain and perpetuate sex-segregated job structures. Finally, they advocated for equal pay for women in an effort to prevent employers from using female labor to undercut the male wage structure. Together, these efforts kept women out of the workforce and ensured that the male breadwinner / female dependent model remained the norm throughout the mid-twentieth century.

The family wage ideology cemented gender disparities; it also helped justify racial prejudices. The family wage made it possible for a working husband to become the sole provider for his wife and children. At the same time, it perpetuated the belief that families that did not conform to the sole-provider model were deviant, lazy, and incompetent. The fact that racial and social prejudice made it harder for members of certain racial groups, particularly black men, to obtain jobs providing a family wage was ignored. Instead, the inability of black husbands to become the sole financial provider for their families was used as evidence of black inferiority. The link between marriage and wage earning helped white men achieve middle-class status, but it simultaneously reduced the social status of black men and their families.

Modern Status Marriages

Under the family wage ideology, both men and women received status from the husband's occupational and financial success, but the reverse was not true. In their 1974 study, "Social Status and the Married Woman," sociologists Marcus Felson and David Knoke demonstrated that the "wife's occupational prestige on [the family's] subjective class was negligible." They demonstrated that only the husband's achievements affected class identification, and today not much has changed.

In the twenty-first century, women continue to derive status from their husbands' success. People may snigger when a man marries his female secretary or when a male doctor marries his female nurse, but such relationships are clichéd rather than taboo. Marriages in which men "marry down" in education or earning power do not harm male status. In fact, these marriages are often status enhancing (for both the husband and wife) because they conform to the traditionally desirable roles of male provider and female dependent. At the same time, a wife's professional success remains largely irrelevant or even detrimental to her husband's social status.

In their 2002 study of class identification of married and employed women and men, sociologists Kazuo Yamaguchi and Yangtao Wang found that when a husband's income is smaller than his wife's, such husbands routinely discount the effect of this income on their class identification. These men would forgo elevating their income status to avoid borrowing their wife's prestige. In explaining this behavior, Yamaguchi and Wang suggested that "borrowing your wife's income status" is psychologically degrading for men because it contradicts the traditional role of the male breadwinner. Yamaguchi and Wang also noted that while higher-earning wives increasingly use their own income in identifying their own class status (a change from the studies conducted in the 1970s), "they do not downplay their spouse's contributions, probably because such a downgrading undermines the traditional role of husbands as family breadwinners."

The psychological effects of male/female income disparities can be a significant factor in marital instability. In their study "When She Brings Home the Status: Wives' Status, Status Leakage and Marital Instability," Canadian professors Alyson Byrne and Julian Barling found that when wives had a higher professional status than their husbands, this often led to resentment and marital instability. Byrne and Barling coined the term *status leakage* to describe what happens when a woman feels her status is lowered on account of her husband's lower level of occupational prestige. They found such women became embarrassed by and resentful of their husbands. These results also have a racial component. The long-standing connection between breadwinner status and black male worth means that status leakage can be especially pronounced for black couples. Studies demonstrate that black women are nearly twice as concerned as white women with their potential husbands' ability to provide a good income and are much less likely to marry unemployed or financially unstable men.

The lopsided gender connection between marriage and status has hindered the creation of egalitarian marriages and stigmatized the role of the supportive male spouse. Men who earn less than their wives feel less secure in these relationships and will compensate by helping less. Studies show that while a wife's economic dependency increases the amount of household labor she performs, a husband's economic dependency reduces his domestic contributions. American men view caretaking as status lowering, thus men who earn less, help less. This doesn't have to be the case.

Women have long derived status from their husband's achievements. If men also believed they benefited from their wives' successes, they might be more willing to assume support-

Julia Letlow.

ive roles. As business school professor Alyson Byrne notes, this is the egalitarian future we want. "When husbands provide their spouses with tangible support — childcare, domestic work, elder support — it signals to the wives, 'I'm supported at home'. . . A dad who takes parental leave is really a great thing, as opposed to a negative thing." Moreover, if men gained status from their wives' successes, the professional achievements of women might also be more widely valued. Instead, women continue to downplay their achievements and hide their ambition behind their roles as wives and mothers. In 2020, Julia Letlow used this age-old strategy when she became the most recent beneficiary of the widow's succession.

Julia ran for office shortly after her husband, Luke Letlow, the congressman-elect for Louisiana's 5th Congressional District seat, died from complications relating to Covid. Like earlier congressional widows, Julia ran as a wife seeking to honor her husband's legacy and continue his work. This strategy worked, and she became the first Republican woman elected to Congress from Louisiana and the only woman among the state's current congressional delegation. In her victory speech, Julia emphasized her domestic obligation, stating, "What was born out of the terrible tragedy of losing my husband, Luke, has become my mission in his honor to carry the torch and serve the good people of Louisiana's 5th District." Julia's political ambitions were aided by her status as a politician's wife.

The recent appointment of Amy Coney Barrett to the Supreme Court provides an even more dramatic example of how marriage and motherhood are still used to make female ambition more acceptable. During the nomination process, Coney Barrett received significant praise for centering her identity as a *mother* before any other personal attribute or accomplishment. When first introducing herself to the nation as the SCOTUS nominee, it is significant that she began by listing all seven of her children. She then added, "While I am a judge, I am better known back home as a room parent, carpool driver, and birthday party planner." As the speech continued, Coney Barrett repeatedly emphasized her role as a wife and mother over all other potential qualifications. In fact, aside from a brief mention of her time clerking for Antonin Scalia, she made no reference to her professional achievements. She appeared to recognize that her nomination to the country's highest court would be most acceptable if it was presented as secondary to her domestic accomplishments.

Marginalizing the Unmarried

One of the greatest costs of linking social, political, and economic status to marriage has been the continuing marginalization of the unmarried. During the fight for same-sex marriage, LGBTQ advocates highlighted the problems with the differential treatment between the married and unmarried. Ultimately, however, the success of the same-sex marriage movement further entrenched the privileged status of marriage.

In the early same-sex marriage case *Perry v. Schwarzenegger*, the court accepted the argument that non-marital relationships "lack the social meaning associated with marriage" and that same-sex marriage bans were effectively "assigning same sex, largely homosexual couples to second class status." In *Obergefell v. Hodges*, the Supreme Court agreed with this assessment and held that only marriage could confer true acceptance of same-sex relationships. Consequently, *Obergefell* reaffirmed the social importance of marriage but simultaneously denigrated the status of the unmarried. As law professor Melissa Murray notes, "According to the [*Obergefell*] majority, life outside of marriage is not only undignified, it is a dismal affair . . . Their intimate lives lack the dignity, transcendence, and purpose that come with knowing that they are a part of a two-person union unlike any other in its importance." The *Obergefell* court is far from alone in this assessment of marriage. As sociologist Andrew Cherlin writes, "Marriage remains the 'ultimate merit badge.'" To be single is still a socially inferior and essentially shameful status.

Today, most forms of discrimination are no longer acceptable, yet it remains largely permissible to deny legal benefits and protections to unmarried people. Title VII of the Civil Rights Act of 1964 does not prohibit workplace discrimination against single people. Similarly, the federal Fair Housing Act of 1968 does not include marital status as a protected class. As a result, the majority of states permit employers to fire single people and landlords to deny them housing. Unmarried couples or families can even be barred from living in entire neighborhoods. Moreover, not only is it permissible to discriminate against the unmarried, it is common. In their research on housing discrimination, Professors Wendy L. Morris, Stacey Sinclair, and Bella M. DePaulo found that landlords repeatedly preferred married people over singles and had no qualms voicing this preference, which they viewed as legitimate and acceptable.

The hundreds of financial benefits available only to the married also remind single people that they are considered less valuable than married people. Admission to a club, charity dinner, or gym is frequently discounted for the married (or at least coupled) and costs significantly less than double the single-person rate. Employers also routinely offer insurance or other employment perks that are cheaper on a per-person basis for couples than for singles. The preference for married people even extends to a belief that their lives are more valuable.

Studies of prisoners show that married prisoners receive more probation than the unmarried and are also less likely to be sentenced to death. A 1967 study of California prisoners noted that "the recommendations of probation agencies and the dispositions of the courts tend to result in the placement of married offenders on probation and the commitment of unmarried offenders to prison." Similarly, a 1980 study focusing on female defendants found that married women were significantly less likely to be imprisoned than their unmarried counterparts. More recently, a 2005 Department of Justice report examining death row inmates also found that these offenders, the ones given the harshest punishment, were typically unmarried.

The unmarried are also less likely to receive lifesaving medical treatment. Research conducted by sociologist Satia Maroatta and public health professor Keren Ladin demonstrated that when married and unmarried patients were equally medically qualified for a transplant, the married patients were more likely to be recommended. Similarly, researcher Joan DelFattore found that single people with cancer were offered less-aggressive treatments by their oncologists than married people. The inevitable conclusion researchers draw from these studies is that the lives of single people are treated as having less worth than the lives of the married.

In his book *Single: Arguments for the Uncoupled*, Michael Cobb, an English professor at the University of Toronto, describes singles as "a hated sexual minority" and argues that they have, essentially, been shamed out of existence. "We live in such a couples-obsessed society that there really are no 'singles' out there — everyone is pre- or post-coupled," says Cobb. He further suggests that even supposedly "pro-single" shows like *Sex and the City* didn't really challenge the elevated status of marriage. "It showed off that you can be single and interesting and buy expensive clothing and go to great parties in New York for a little while but eventually you are going to grow up. Eventually, you're going to wisen up, put a ring on it and go forward and be coupled and move to Connecticut. We aren't going to pathologize you for playing around for a protracted amount of time, but eventually you're going to have to settle. And the marker of success, the end of the romantic story, is [marriage]."

The social and cultural preference for marriage has obvious negative effects for single people, but it also harms the married. A desire to retain marriage's preferential status is one of the most cited explanations for why people remain in unhappy marriages. In an illuminating Facebook thread, journalist and former academic Anne Helen Peterson asked her followers, "What keeps feminist bourgeoise women from leaving shitty spouses?" Peterson then received hundreds of responses, many of which focused on the status benefits of marriage. One respondent noted that it may be "superficial," but the "public shame" should not be "discounted" and added that the proliferation of social media has further increased the social benefits of marriage because "so much of the wins online are connected to marriage." A second woman responded to Peterson's inquiry, writing, "Oh man reading these comments has really reminded me how being in a relationship is so socially desirable many people would rather be completely and utterly miserable in one than even a tiny bit unhappy and single." A third described multiple "friends (who have the means to leave) who seem to value marriage more than their happiness." She then added, "I think it has something to do with the class privilege they occupy and a lifestyle that depends upon doing things with spouses."

Many of the women who responded to Peterson's inquiry noted that the social status attached to marriage can be compounded by race. For example, one woman answered Peterson's question with the statement, "Proximity to whiteness," implying that marriage provides people of color with greater racial acceptance by the white community. Another respondent expanded on this idea, stating that "for white families there is a cultural affinity for 'the more perfect union.' The constant seeking of status, approval . . . The individual family unit is fetishized as the ultimate expression of success. So yes the proximity to whiteness as [the above respondent] points out, but I think it is immersion in whiteness, the desire to remain immersed in whiteness, to never be associated with anything else. I'm a relatively bougie white lady and I'm in a good relationship but the idea of that falling apart scares the shit out of me and I reckon part of that fear is a sense of cultural failing. That my family wouldn't 'look like it's supposed to' . . . I could make it work if I had to, but it is still terrifying and a big piece of that is because I'm white."

Historically, the unmarried were pitied, reviled, and relegated to the social bottom. Today, that social ostracization continues. For many Americans, marriage remains a defining feature of a person's worth. It is therefore unsurprising that people continue to enter into and remain in loveless marriages. Zsa Zsa Gabor once quipped, "Getting divorced because you don't love a man is almost as silly as getting married because you do." As Gabor recognized, in America the social penalties for the unmarried remain high. For many men and women, avoiding this stigma is a good enough reason to marry.

chapter four

The Marriage Defense

But if they cannot contain, let them marry:
for it is better to marry than to burn.

— I CORINTHIANS 7:9

One Friday night in October 1884, William Ward and Margaret O'Rourke attended a ball in the small town of Mount Vernon, New York, forty miles north of New York City. William and Margaret were likely already acquainted. In fact, they may have known each other for some time, because when William suggested going back to his rooms, Margaret readily agreed.

William lived in Mrs. Butterfield's boardinghouse. This was a reputable business that did not condone non-marital sex, so when Mrs. Butterfield discovered Margaret in William's room the next morning, she was horrified. She informed the couple she was not running *that* kind of establishment and promptly kicked them both out. Mortified, Margaret sought refuge with her friends. She told them about her night with William and their subsequent discovery by Mrs. Butterfield. The friends then informed her father, who had William arrested. After the arrest, Margaret was questioned about her night with William. She admitted to having sex but claimed she only acquiesced after William proposed. Based on this testimony, William was charged with seduction under promise of marriage. He was then brought before a judge and given a choice. He could go to jail, or he could marry. Not surprisingly, William chose the latter. A minister was called into the courtroom, and the couple was promptly wed.

A century and a half later, it is impossible to know what really happened the night of the Mount Vernon ball. Perhaps William did propose and would have married Margaret without any legal threats. It is also possible, as Margaret's father clearly suspected, that William said what he needed to say to get Margaret into bed and that he had no intention of following through with his promise. It is even conceivable that William never said anything about marriage and Margaret fabricated the alleged proposal to save her reputation or to trap William. We can't know what truly happened between William and Margaret the night of the ball, but what is clear is that by marrying Margaret, William avoided prison.

Sex and the Unmarried

For most of US history, only the married could, legally, have sex. Fornication, defined as voluntary sexual intercourse between unmarried parties, was criminalized, and this was done intentionally to encourage marriage. As the influential eighteenth-century English philosopher William Paley explained, "The male part of the species will not undertake the encumbrance, expense, and restraint of married life, if they can gratify their [sexual] passions at a cheaper price; and they will undertake anything rather than not gratify them." Paley believed the only way to convince men to marry was to make the price of non-marital sex extremely high. Early American laws sanctioning monetary suits against male fornicators reflected this idea.

Initially, fornication was punished through two types of legal actions, suits for seduction and suits for breach of promise. Seduction suits were brought by an unmarried woman's father against the alleged seducer for the economic injury he suffered as a result of his daughter's unintended pregnancy. Many of these

Before the Seduction, by William Hogarth, 1731.

suits were brought by working-class fathers against higher-class men, often employers (or their sons), who had taken advantage of the young women in their care. Seduction suits were a way of discouraging such behavior.

Breach of promise actions, unlike seduction suits, were brought by the woman against her former fiancé and were based on the presumed economic injury resulting from a failed engagement. As these suits recognized, marriage was essential to a woman's economic security, and a broken engagement, with its taint of impropriety (it was frequently presumed, often correctly, that many jilted women were no longer virgins), affected a woman's potential marital prospects and her future economic well-being.

By the mid-nineteenth century, the distinctions between the two causes of action had collapsed. Pregnancy began to feature in breach of promise suits as grounds for increased damages, and

The Spurned Bride by Eduard Swoboda.

a promise of marriage, which induced a woman to consent to sexual intercourse (regardless of pregnancy), became a common feature of seduction suits. The emotional suffering caused by the man's behavior also became a feature of these suits, and the rise of industrialization transformed them still further.

As young women left the safety of their rural communities and moved to the cities for work, they became increasingly vulnerable to sexual exploitation and assault. Increasingly, seduction cases were brought by these young working-class women after a rape by friends or other acquaintances. Such women had not consented to sex, but because rape between dating partners was rarely punished, seduction suits were often the only way to hold these men accountable. However, the remedy these women wanted was not money, it was marriage.

Martha Olatka's complaint against Michael Polokoff is typical of such cases. In 1914, Martha was a twenty-three-year-old domestic servant. In May of that year, she began dating Michael Polokoff, a twenty-four-year-old immigrant laborer. For ten

Bell Time, by Winslow Homer.

months, Polokoff took Martha out twice a week and repeatedly told her he wished to marry her. He also constantly pressured her for sex. As Martha later told the police, during their dates, Polokoff would try to pull up her clothes, touch her body, and kiss and hug her. Martha testified that she vigorously repulsed these efforts but that on the night of the "seduction," William found her alone in her cousin's house and physically overpowered her. According to Martha, "[Polokoff] came to me and he locked the door, and he put me in the bed. I started to holler, and he closed my mouth, and he said, 'Don't holler,' and he pulled up my clothes and then he had connection with me . . . I tried to stop him, but I couldn't; he said, 'Don't you worry, I am going to marry you.'" After the first assault, Polokoff raped Martha on three additional occasions, each time telling her, "I won't marry you if you won't let me."

By July 1915, Martha was pregnant and desperately trying to convince Polokoff to marry her. After he repeatedly refused, she warned him, "If you don't marry me, I'll take you to court."

Polokoff didn't believe her, but one week later, Martha filed criminal charges. Polokoff was then brought to the Manhattan District Attorney's Office and threatened with imprisonment. At that point, he finally agreed to marry Martha, but begged for a little more time. According to Martha, "He came to me, and he was crying, and said I should give him a chance of one month to think it over." Martha unwisely took pity on Polokoff. Three days after agreeing to marriage, Polokoff came to Martha boasting, "I fooled the court, and I fool you; I am not afraid of the court; they did nothing." He then disappeared, along with $36 Martha had given him to pay the rent on his plumbing office. Shortly thereafter, Martha miscarried. For weeks she was too sick to take further action, but December 18, 1915, Martha had recovered enough to appear in magistrate's court and have Polokoff charged with seduction. On January 19, 1916, Polokoff was arrested.

At a time when women had little legal recourse against sexual assault, forced marriage protected them, and their children, from abandonment and destitution. It was also, unquestionably, a punishment for the men. As law professor Melissa Murray has written, "Though marriage did not require the physical deprivations of incarceration, it nonetheless deprived the defendant . . . of other liberties by imposing upon him a particular set of burdens and responsibilities — fidelity, sobriety, responsibility, wage-earning — that he could not cast off lightly." Consequently, by the reasoning of the times, the problem with using marriage as a punishment for rape was not that it was ineffective or undesired but that this remedy was not available to all victims.

In late-nineteenth- and early-twentieth-century America, interracial marriage was illegal in many states. As a result, marriage could not be used to punish white men who seduced

/ sexually assaulted black women. It was this disparity in the availability of the marriage remedy that convinced many civil rights leaders to oppose anti-miscegenation laws. In the 1920s, civil rights leaders, like Archibald Grimke, president of the American Negro Academy, argued that the best way to stop illicit sex was to legalize interracial marriage. According to Grimke, "When it comes to a [white] man marrying a colored woman, he does not want to do it," and as long as such laws were in place he could not be compelled to "do it." As Grimke noted, anti-miscegenation laws prevented black women from being as "sacredly guarded by law and public opinion against the sexual passion and pursuit of the white man as is the white woman." NAACP president James Wheldon Johnson made a similar observation. He labeled these prohibitions the "magna charta [*sic*] of concubinage and bastardry [*sic*]."

An additional limitation of the marriage remedy was that it was only available to virgins. Nineteenth-century jurists believed that once a woman consented to non-marital sex with one man, she possessed a character for unchastity and could be assumed to have consented to sex in all other instances as well. In the 1838 case *People v. Abbot*, the New York court expressed this view of female chastity when it sanctimoniously declared, "An isolated instance of criminal connection [fornication] does not make a common prostitute . . . [I]t only makes a prostitute." Only a chaste woman could accuse a man of a sexual crime. Tellingly, this assumption regarding sex and honesty did not apply to male witnesses. In the 1895 case *State v. Sibley*, which concerned the defendant's alleged rape of his twelve-year-old stepdaughter, the Missouri Supreme Court noted, "It is a matter of common knowledge that the bad character of a man for chastity does not even in the remotest degree affect his character for truth, when based upon that alone, while it does that of a woman."

Widespread Bigamy

The marriage defense provided protection against criminal charges of fornication and seduction. It also, ironically, protected against charges of bigamy. In nineteenth-century America, bigamy was a crime, but if a man or woman lived with someone as their spouse, meaning the parties assumed all the traditional rights and obligations of marriage, the law would assume the couple was legally capable of marriage. The justification for presuming the validity of a bigamous marriage was twofold. First, the law presumes innocence, meaning courts would assume a person claiming to be married was married. Second, even if courts suspected bigamy, they still supported these illegal "marriages" as preferable to legal divorce. The result, as Professor Lawrence Friedman has written, was that "unhappy spouses would divorce with their feet." They would physically separate, often by moving to a new city or state, and then start over with a new husband or wife. If the new, bigamous marriage looked like a valid marriage, judges would treat it as valid. Most bigamy prosecutions were limited to brazen or fraudulent acts.

A typical bigamy prosecution was that of Fredrick A. Smith. In 1897, Smith was charged with bigamy after he abandoned his first wife and began "housekeeping" with another woman a short distance away. The first Mrs. Smith quickly located her husband (and her furniture) and had him arrested for bigamy. The 1890 bigamy prosecution of Horace Knapp is similar. Horace Knapp was a California miner who met Annie Gale through a matrimonial advertisement. Knapp described himself as a "good fellow, with means and prospects," and Gale eagerly responded to his advertisement. The two met in person and quickly married. Shortly thereafter, Annie received an anonymous note. It read:

Mrs. Knapp, your husband has another wife living not far from you. He has three children whom he has deserted. He married you to get whatever money you had or could acquire. She is innocent and knows nothing of him having married you. Don't bother her, poor thing; she has a hard enough time to feed her babies.

After confirming the truth of the note, Gale had Knapp arrested for bigamy. However, such prosecutions were rare. Most bigamists were never prosecuted.

By the mid-nineteenth century, bigamy was so widespread that many matrimonial advertisers — men seeking mail-order brides — felt they needed to specifically note if they were not open to such marriages. An 1867 issue of *The Miner*, reprinted in the *Montana Post*, included such a stipulation. It read: "Wanted — a wife, by a young, temperate, industrious miner. No old maids or fast widows need apply." A "fast widow" was a married woman looking for a new husband.

Historian Beverly Schwartzberg's fascinating study of nineteenth-century widows' pensions also reveals the extraordinary prevalence of bigamy. During her research, Schwartzberg uncovered thousands of pension cases in which more than one woman (sometimes many, many more) claimed to be the widow of a single Civil War soldier. She similarly discovered it was also common for the women to have multiple husbands. The example of Amelia Van Gedler and William Bacon is illustrative.

William and Amelia married in 1865 in Southport, New York. Six months later, William deserted Amelia and "married" a woman named Cordelia. When asked "how he could marry again without getting a divorce," William told his friend, "Lots of them did . . . that." After William's desertion, Amelia also

Yours for Business and Success...

Charles M. Wright

...EXPERT...

Pension ɑ Claim Attorney

Fifteen Years' Experience.
Best of References.

THE EXPERT.   WAPELLO, IOWA.

The business card of one of the many attorneys special-
izing in pension claims, circa 1895. Civil War pensions
became so legally complicated that entire legal practices
were created just to handle these claims.

"remarried," and after her second husband died, she remarried
again. Then, after her third husband died, Amelia learned that
William was also deceased so, because Amelia was now single,
she applied for a pension as William's widow.

Bigamy allowed spouses like William and Amelia to elude
America's draconian divorce prohibitions. It also protected them
against charges of fornication or adultery. Both of these benefits
were especially important for abused wives. The pension claim
of Civil War veteran William Butler shows how bigamy helped
protect abused women.

William Butler had multiple wives. He was also a violent
man. His pension claim reveals that his first wife, Marion, left
him due to "ill treatment," and although the record is silent as
to the details of Marion's abuse, the testimony of his third wife,
Nannie, indicates it was likely horrific. In her pension interview, Nannie testified that she left Butler "after he removed
every stick of furniture from the house and locked her and
her children in." She further testified that, had it not been for
neighbors, they would probably have died of exposure. Marion's
bigamous remarriage helped her avoid Nannie's fate. It gave her
the economic support to leave Butler and protected her against

criminal charges of adultery. Years later, when the pension examiner inspected Marion's claim, he decided she was eligible for Butler's pension because her bigamous second (and then third) marriage meant she was not living in "open and notorious adulterous cohabitation."

Spousal Privilege

The criminal defense benefits of marriage helped alleviate some of the injustice caused by women's inequality and powerlessness. Unfortunately, the marriage defense also incentivized highly problematic and dangerous marriages. The spousal testimonial privilege, which prevents spouses from testifying against each other, is one obvious example. This privilege derives from the law of coverture, which treated the husband and wife as one person. Under coverture, a married woman had no separate legal identity from her husband. This meant, among other things, that she could not testify against him. It also meant that marrying a witness, or even a victim, could be an effective criminal defense strategy.

In his 1827 treatise *Rationale of Judicial Evidence*, the famous English philosopher and jurist Jeremy Bentham railed against the marital testimonial privilege because it allowed a person to convert her home into a "den of thieves" and ensured every married individual "one safe and unquestionable and ever ready accomplice for every imaginable crime." Bentham's fears were valid, but they were unpersuasive. In fact, even after the rule of coverture was replaced with the rule of love, support for the privilege did not disappear. Instead, the justification changed. Now courts upheld the privilege as necessary to marital harmony and declared that marital relations would become frayed if husbands and wives were forced to testify against the other. The continuing strength of the testimonial privilege is clearly demonstrated in the 1903 Texas murder trial of A. J. Moore.

The case began on a warm Sunday night, shortly after evening church services had concluded. One of the attendees, Matt Hunt, began to walk home with Susie Jones. Susie was A. J. Moore's girlfriend, and Moore objected. When Susie ignored him, he slapped her across the face. Hunt intervened, and he and Moore began shouting at each other. Eventually, Susie left with Hunt, while an enraged Moore followed them. Shortly after the couple reached Susie's house, Moore shot Hunt in the head. Susie was the only witness. Moore was subsequently arrested and the state expected Susie to testify. However, on the eve of trial, Susie and Moore were married. The following day, Moore argued that because Susie was now his wife, she could not be forced to testify. The court agreed. Although the Moores' marriage was only hours old, the court ruled that the prosecution could not compel Susie's testimony. According to the court, "It makes no difference at what time the relation of husband and wife begins . . . When the marriage ceremony is performed, no matter what the motive was or may be, the witness thenceforward becomes the lawful wife of the defendant, and is prohibited . . . from testifying against her husband."

Protecting Domestic Violence

Marriage allowed Moore to silence Susie's testimony. It also, likely, protected him from prosecution for domestic abuse. Moore was a violent man. He had hit Susie in public and murdered the man who tried to protect her. Once married, it is almost certain this abuse continued. However, after Moore became Susie's husband, it became exceedingly unlikely he would ever be punished for domestic violence.

A 1782 caricature by James Gillray.

Historically, husbands had the right to physically chastise their wives. A husband was legally responsible for a wife's conduct, and this gave him the right to control her behavior, including with physical force or violence. This right of chastisement was sometimes known as the Rule of Thumb, in reference to the English common-law rule that a husband had the authority to beat his wife with a "rod not thicker than his thumb."

The right of chastisement, combined with coverture's prohibition on suits between spouses, meant husbands could not be prosecuted for most domestic violence. Abusing one's wife became a privilege of marriage. *The Comic Blackstone*, a satirical

1846 examination of the common law, mocked the chastisement right while simultaneously acknowledging its appeal:

> By the old law, a husband might give his wife moderate correction . . . but it is declared in black and white that he may not beat her black and blue, though the civil law allowed any man on whom a woman had bestowed her hand, to bestow his fists upon her at his own discretion. The common people, who are much attached to the common law, still exert the privilege of beating their wives . . . and a woman in the lower ranks of life, if she falls in love with a man, is liable, after marriage, to be a good deal struck by him.

By the 1870s, women's rights advocates began citing the chastisement right as one of the reasons women needed the vote. Women's newspapers, such as the *Woman's Journal*, published stories of wife beatings, murder, rape, and incest to emphasize the frequency of such abuse and the need for reform. As one column in the *Woman's Journal* noted, "The instances here reported are only a few of many similar ones which crowd our daily papers and which show the need for a redeemed public sentiment in regard to this great crime." Women's rights advocates cited these gruesome reports as proof that husbands could not be trusted to protect women's interests and that women needed their own right to participate in the enactment and enforcement of the law.

The increased attention to the problem of domestic violence did not lead to suffrage, but it did change the justification for the policy of judicial non-interference. The right of chastisement was replaced with a concern for marital harmony. The 1886 North Carolina Supreme Court case *State v. Edens* exemplified this new justification. In *Edens*, the court described the marital

Suffragist Margaret Foley distributing the *Woman's Journal and Suffrage News*.

home as an idealized private realm ruled by love and potentially harmed by outside interference. The court wrote:

> [The law] drops the curtain upon scenes of domestic life, preferring not to take cognizance of what transpires within that circle, to the exposure of them in a public prosecution. It presumes that acts of wrong committed in passion will be followed by contrition and atonement in a cooler moment, and forgiveness will blot it out of memory. So, too, the harsh and cruel word that sends a pang to the sensitive heart may be recalled, and relations that should never have been interrupted by an unkind or unwarranted expression again restored.

Non-interference in the name of marital harmony quickly became an accepted feature of the criminal justice system. Instead of punishing domestic abusers, family courts encouraged reconciliation. They also insisted family conflict, including violence, should remain private. State legislatures helped further this goal by creating separate family and juvenile courts. These courts guaranteed that cases involving family violence were heard outside of the traditional criminal system. As law professor Reva Seigel notes, the changes ensured that the "ancient prerogative of marriage, chastisement did not die an easy death." Rather, these changes re-legitimized and more deeply entrenched the practice of judicial non-interference. The history of marital rape is similar.

Marital Rape

Traditionally, the right to have sex with one's wife was one of the benefits of marriage. This was because marital sex was the only permissible form of intercourse and because a wife could not, legally, say no. The idea that marital rape was a legal impossibility originated in a seventeenth-century treatise authored by Lord Matthew Hale, the chief justice of England. In this treatise, Hale wrote, "The husband cannot be guilty of a rape committed by himself upon his lawful wife, for by their mutual matrimonial consent and contract the wife hath given up herself in this kind unto her husband, which she cannot retract." Hale provided no precedent for his theory of perpetual consent, but it was readily accepted into the common law. Marriage became an absolute defense to rape.

By the nineteenth century, a husband's right of sexual access had expanded to include the right to prevent his wife from having sex with others. This meant, if a woman committed adultery, her husband could sue her lover for "criminal conversation" and receive monetary damages. He also had the right to recapture, restrain, and confine his wife to keep her from committing adultery and the right to seek a writ of habeas corpus (a document ordering a person's release) against any person who kept his wife from him. The husband's sexual monopoly over his wife even gave him a defense to murder. The 1859 murder trial of Daniel Sickles established this "heat of passion defense."

Daniel Sickles was a New York City congressman who murdered the district attorney of New York after discovering he was having an affair with his wife. At trial, Sickles claimed a loss of control due to intense romantic jealousy. His attorney likened this argument to the already accepted defense of temporary insanity. According to Sickles's attorney, in such cases, deadly violence must be excused. "To kill in the name of jealousy is merely obedience to the will of nature." Shockingly, the jury agreed, and Sickles was acquitted. Ten years later, the heat of passion defense became the core issue in the even more sensational New York murder trial of Daniel McFarland.

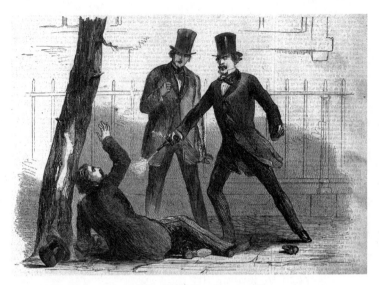

Harper's Weekly engraving of Daniel Sickles shooting Key.

In 1857, Daniel McFarland married Abby Sage. McFarland told Abby he was a successful lawyer and "a man of temperate habits, of the purest morals." However, neither was true. Shortly after their marriage, Abby discovered that McFarland was a broke land speculator and an alcoholic. Three months after their wedding, McFarland pawned Abby's jewelry to pay their bills. He also forced her to become an actress to support the family, and he began hurting her. Then, after ten years of marriage and abuse, Abby met Albert Richardson.

Albert Richardson was a journalist living in the same boardinghouse as the McFarlands. He was intelligent and kind, and he and Abby quickly became friends. McFarland grew jealous of this friendship, and one evening McFarland came home to find Abby standing by Richardson's door and flew into a terrible rage. He beat Abby throughout the night and into the next day, taking breaks only to go "to the nearest bar-room to drink, and then [to] com[e] in still more furious." Eventually, after more

Abby McFarland and Albert Richardson.

than a full day of abuse, Abby told McFarland she was leaving. Recalling that night, Abby stated:

> As mildly and firmly as I possibly could, I began to talk with him. I told him decidedly that I should leave him forever; that I had borne with patience for many years great outrages from him; that he had made my life miserable, and had often put me in great dread of my life; that I could not endure it any longer; that by his outrageous conduct for the two days past, and by the language he had used when he found me at Mr. Richardson's door, he had added the last drop to my cup of endurance, and I should go away from him at once.

Abby left McFarland. In response, McFarland shot Richardson. Richardson survived this attack, and Abby filed for divorce. Sixteen months later, the length of time needed to establish residency in Indiana (one of the few states where divorce was

First day of the McFarland trial — scene in the courtroom.

permissible), the divorce was granted. Unfortunately, as Abby and Albert were preparing to marry, McFarland shot Richardson a second time. This time, the shot was fatal. Richardson died, and McFarland was arrested for murder.

McFarland admitted to killing Richardson. The only issue at trial was whether he had the right to do so. McFarland's lawyers argued that when Abby left McFarland, it made him crazy. They contended that when he shot Richardson, McFarland was acting under an "ungovernable impulse, uncontrolled by reason," and thus was neither morally nor legally responsible for Richardson's death. The jury agreed. After deliberating for less than an hour, McFarland was acquitted. Tellingly, the public supported this result. Despite the abuse, most Americans blamed Richardson for stealing Abby away. McFarland was viewed as an honorable man who only did what love compelled him to do.

A Loophole for Statutory Rapists

Marriage provided husbands with a defense to rape and murder. It also became a defense to child sexual abuse. Historically, statutory rape laws only forbade sexual intercourse with a female under the age of ten or twelve (it varied slightly by state). Then, in the 1890s, social reformers began working to increase the age of consent. By the 1920s, all but one state had raised it to sixteen. Nevertheless, there were two glaring exceptions to the new statutory rape laws. The first was that they only applied to virgins. The second was marriage. Despite growing concerns regarding child sexual abuse, marriage remained a loophole for men wishing to have sex with children.

One of the most famous examples of the child sex loophole was the marriage of Edward "Daddy" Browning and Frances "Peaches" Heenan. "Daddy" and "Peaches" were the couple's revealing nicknames for each other. The two met in the spring of 1926 when Browning was a fifty-one-year-old multimillionaire and Frances was a fifteen-year-old high school student. Browning liked young girls. Long before he met Frances, there were allegations Browning had molested his own adopted daughter. Then, as he and Frances started "dating," Browning came under increasing legal scrutiny.

Vincent Pisarra, the superintendent of the New York Society for the Prevention of Cruelty to Children, believed Browning's interest in Frances was child abuse. He attempted to end the relationship by filing suit in New York Children's Court and having Frances's mother declared unfit. This would have invalidated her ability to consent to the marriage. Unfortunately, Browning discovered Pisarra's plan and thwarted it by marrying Frances one month after meeting her. Once married, Browning had the legal right to have sex with Frances.

Frances "Peaches" Heenan.

The Browning marriage lasted less than a year, and it ruined Frances's life. After a much-publicized divorce, in which Frances was vilified and denied a fair share of the marital assets, she had a short-lived career as a vaudeville actress and then three additional, unsuccessful, marriages. Frances died at age forty-six after a slip and fall in her bathroom.

The Married Prostitute

Marriage shielded husbands from criminal prosecution for physical abuse, sexual abuse, and even murder. However, the marriage defense was not limited to men. Women also used marriage as a defense strategy, most commonly against charges of prostitution. In fact, during the late nineteenth century, marriage was such an effective defense that prostitutes could boldly advertise their services simply by including the word *marriage*. Consider the following solicitation: "A discreet young lady, cosy home, appreciates meeting generous gentleman, matrimony." Few readers would have thought this "discreet young lady" was looking for marriage. As a different advertiser explained, "The [newspaper editors] know I don't want to marry, and most of those who answer know it too."

Nineteenth-century prostitutes were able to advertise their services and circumvent the law by simply including the word *marriage*. Then, in the early twentieth century, this leniency disappeared as Congress became increasingly concerned about the immigration of foreign prostitutes and their use of marriage to evade immigration restrictions. Initially, Congress attempted to address the problem of foreign prostitutes through the Immigration Act of 1907. The act barred foreign women from entering the US for "immoral purposes." One year later, the Supreme Court decided *U.S. v. Bitty* and upheld the act's "immoral purposes" ban, but also confirmed that this prohibition could be circumvented through marriage.

Bitty involved the arrest of Englishman John Bitty after he entered the United States with Violet Sterling, a twenty-one-year-old Englishwoman whose travel documents identified her as Betty Bitty. When questioned by the police, Bitty told the following story: "The girl [Sterling] worked for me [selling cigarettes] in London . . . [W]hen I started for New York she begged me not to leave her. I engaged passage for her as my niece, as I thought that would look better. I had taken a fatherly interest in her." The police did not believe Bitty's story and charged him with violating section three of the 1907

Immigration Act, "import[ing] or attempt[ing] to import, into the United States, any alien woman or girl for the purpose of prostitution or for any other immoral purpose." Bitty objected to the charge. He noted that Sterling was not a prostitute, but the court held this made no difference. As the court explained, Bitty brought Sterling into the United States to "live with him as his concubine, that is, in illicit intercourse, not under the sanction of a valid or legal marriage." According to the court, this satisfied the act's immoral purposes provision. The important difference was not between a "concubine" and a "prostitute," but between a wife and all other women.

The 1907 Immigration Act also created the Dillingham Commission. The purpose of this commission was to conduct a wide-ranging investigation of US immigration practices, including the immigration of prostitutes. In 1911, Congress published the Dillingham Commission's report and confirmed that marriage was routinely used to circumvent the 1907 act's immoral purposes provision. The report noted that, initially, immigration officials had attempted to bar foreign prostitutes by identifying them based on physical characteristics such as their dress or speech but that these efforts were abandoned after one hapless immigration inspector stopped the wife of a rich and important citizen and nearly accused her of prostitution. The woman was gaudily dressed and unrefined, but she was not a prostitute. Luckily the mistake was caught before the woman discovered why she had been briefly detained. Nevertheless, the mishap highlighted the danger of using appearance or manner to identify prostitutes. Afterward, female entry determinations were primarily based on marital status. Single women attempting to enter the US alone or with a male partner were turned away as likely prostitutes; married women were almost always granted entry.

The Dillingham report confirmed, marriage was the key to evading the 1907 act. However, in discussing the entry of foreign prostitutes the report also stoked "white slavery" fears. At the time, there was a widespread belief that large numbers of unwilling women were being tricked into sex work through false promises of marriage made by foreign or other racially "inferior" men. In 1907, a *Los Angeles Times* article titled "Jewish Girls Are Sacrificed: Sensational Disclosures from Chicago Ghetto" claimed, "Some [Jewish procurers] seek the company of Jewish maidens with avowed intention of honorable marriage. Others actually marry the girls and then force them to lead dissolute lives. Many . . . have married dozens of girls under various names and disguises." In 1909, *McClure's Magazine* ran a similar article titled "Daughters of the Poor." According to this article, "A network of Austrian, Russian, and Hungarian Jews dealt in women" and warned that these "lonely and poverty stricken girls . . . are very easily secured by promise of marriage." The Dillingham report appeared to confirm these fears. The report noted:

> The Jews often import or harbor Russian, Hungarian, Polish or German women, doubtlessly usually of their own race . . . There are large numbers of Jews scattered through the United States, although mainly located in New York and Chicago, who seduce and keep girls. Some of them are engaged in importation.

Historian Nancy Cott notes that it was easy for Americans "to believe that 'racially' different and non-Christian groups were likely to commit such grotesquery." She writes, "Both Asians and Jews — the latter via the Old Testament — were tainted by association with polygamy . . . Also, both Jews and Asians

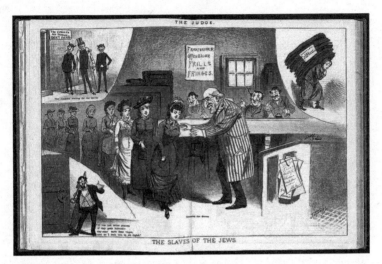

The Slaves of the Jews by J. A. Wales (a known anti-Semitic cartoonist), published in *Judge* magazine in 1882.

in their home cultures used arranged marriages, in which overt economic bargaining and kinship networks beyond the marrying pair played acknowledged parts."

The racism underlying early-twentieth-century marriage trafficking fears was obvious. Nevertheless, there is little question that marriage was used to bring willing, and possibly unwilling, sex workers into the United States. As one Marseilles madam told the commission's agents, "All the bunch that I know [referring to the male facilitators], marry their girls. If the girl is young, you then have no trouble."

Marriage helped foreign prostitutes enter the United States. It also helped them avoid deportation after entry. Under an 1855 federal statute, the foreign wives of American citizens received automatic citizenship. Any American man could marry a foreign-born (though not Asian) woman and remove her from the reach of immigration laws. As a result, marriage quickly became a common and effective tactic foreign prostitutes used

Men of the New Immigration Commission.

to avoid deportation. As the Dillingham report noted, "One of the great difficulties encountered in the deportation of alien prostitutes, has been the contraction of marriages to citizens of the United States as soon as warrant proceedings have been instituted." To illustrate this problem, the report highlighted one New York City police detective's unsuccessful efforts to deport "Jane Doe."

Doe was arrested for solicitation, but shortly after her arrest, she married an American citizen. According to Doe, the man "got 'dead stuck' on me, because I appeared to be a nice girl . . . I know how to behave, when necessary." When the detective arrived to order her deportation, Doe showed him her marriage certificate. She then boasted that the poor sucker who married her wasn't even around anymore. She told the detective, "I couldn't live with that man . . . he isn't making enough money. I don't want to go into the dressmaking business and earn $8 or $9 a week when I can make that every day on Broadway." Once

Doe proved she was the wife of an American citizen, the detective was forced to release her. The officer concluded his interview with the commission noting, "Almost every night I see the said Jane Doe (now Mrs. Doe) soliciting on Broadway and taking men to hotels in that vicinity."

Women like Mrs. Doe convinced lawmakers that the connection between marriage and citizenship was promoting prostitution and degrading marriage. Responding to these concerns, Congress passed the Immigration Act of 1917. This statute decreed "that the marriage to an American citizen of a female of the sexually immoral classes, the exclusion or deportation of which is prescribed by this Act, shall not invest such female with United States citizenship if the marriage of such an alien female shall be solemnized after her arrest or after the commission of acts which make her liable to deportation under this Act." The 1917 act ensured that marriage was no longer a defense to the deportation of foreign prostitutes. Nevertheless, it did not portend the end of the marriage defense. In fact, it proved to be the exception.

The Marriage Defense's Many Guises Today

Today, the connection between marriage and criminal defense continues. This is true for acts that are no longer criminalized, like seduction and breach of promise to marry, and for crimes like domestic violence and child abuse, which are now more vigorously enforced.

For example, a recent "offer" during the COVID-19 pandemic from the Robeson County, North Carolina, sheriff's office demonstrates the ongoing criminalization of jilters. In this "Pre-Valentine's Day special," the department offered to arrest "your ex" for Valentine's Day:

If you have an ex-Valentine with an outstanding warrant who is playing hide-and-seek now is the time to enjoy this offer. The weekend special offers a set of limited-edition platinum bracelets, free face mask, free hand sanitizer, along with free transportation provided by a state-certified chauffeur, free glamour headshot, a one-night minimum stay in our luxurious, freshly painted, 5-star accommodations with 24/7 security, and a unique Valentine's dinner.

Jilting is no longer a crime, yet the Robeson police department was specifically targeting jilters for criminal punishment. Other historic morality crimes, such as fornication and cohabitation, also continue to have criminal repercussions. Some of the most common examples are parole restrictions.

In 2004, North Carolina refused to supervise the parole of Melissa Sheridan because she was cohabitating with her boyfriend in violation of North Carolina's no-longer-enforced 1805 anti-cohabitation statute. To remain with her partner in North Carolina, Sheridan was told to marry. Terry Gootee, judicial district manager with the 5th Judicial District's Division of Community Corrections, explained the parole decision, stating, "We cannot allow that person to break the law." Other states have issued similar parole denials. In 2006, West Virginia refused to release William Stanley because he planned to cohabitate with his fiancée. Stanley remained incarcerated until he was finally paroled to a religious program that required daily prayer sessions and memorization of religious materials. Similarly, in 2007, a Texas court issued a parole condition for Briane Woods prohibiting her from residing with any person other than a spouse or blood relative. The court justified this parole condition by claiming Woods's mother's out-of-wedlock childbearing, and Woods's own decision to not "marry the father of her one-year-old child and her unborn baby," contributed to her criminal behavior.

Sexual Harassment and the Marriage Defense

The punishment of non-marital sex also continues through a system of civil regulations. Sexual harassment regulations are the most prominent example. These rules were created to reduce gender discrimination in the workplace. However, many go beyond their stated anti-discrimination objectives to regulate sex, and sexuality more generally. Many employers now prohibit sexual conduct that would not amount to sexual harassment. At the same time, sexual harassment is becoming even harder to discern, and this makes employers even more inclined to regulate employee sex. As law professors Melissa Murray and Karen Tani write, today "few sexual encounters are presumptively permissible or impermissible." Instead, "the legitimacy of every encounter turns on consent. But even (and perhaps especially) in this 'yes means yes' era, expressions of consent are subject to interpretation, and thus disagreement." Regulation of such encounters is then further complicated by the fact that workplace romance is common and often highly successful.

Workplace romance statistics show that while it is often assumed most people meet online, in reality more people meet their spouse in the workplace than on an app. A 2023 *Forbes* survey "found that 43% of those who date a colleague end up marrying them." Nevertheless, the fear of sexual harassment suits means employers are now regulating a wider range of sexual behavior and often prohibiting employee relationships altogether. Two recent cases concerning non-marital sex by public employees, *Seegmiller v. LaVerkin City* and *Anderson v. City of LaVergne*, illustrate the growing regulation of employee sex.

Seegmiller concerned the non-marital sexual conduct of Sharon Johnson. Johnson was a Utah police officer involved in a contentious divorce. During an out-of-town police training conference, Johnson had "a brief affair with an officer from another department who was also attending the conference." When Johnson's estranged husband learned of the affair, he contacted her employer, the LaVerkin Police Department, and told them she had been raped. Johnson denied being raped, and no disciplinary action was taken against her lover. This inaction enraged Johnson's husband, who reported to the city council that Johnson was having an affair with the police chief. While investigating this allegation (which the husband later recanted), the city council learned about Johnson's conference relationship. Johnson was issued a formal reprimand based on a provision in the law enforcement code of ethics requiring an officer to "keep [her] private life unsullied as an example to all and [to] behave in a manner that does not bring discredit to [the officer] or [the] agency." She was also warned that further violations of the professional code would result in "additional discipline up to and including termination." After receiving this reprimand, Johnson sued the city. She argued that punishment for off-duty private conduct was a violation of her constitutional rights. The *Seegmiller* court disagreed and held that her reprimand was constitutional.

In *Anderson*, two employees of the LaVergne, Tennessee, police department, Michael Anderson, a police officer, and Lisa Lewis, an administrative assistant, began a romantic relationship. When the police chief learned of their relationship, he became concerned that "intra-office dating between employees of different ranks . . . might lead to sexual harassment claims against the department." In response, he issued an administrative order directing Anderson and Lewis to "cease all contact with each other" outside of the workplace. The couple ignored the order and continued their relationship. Shortly thereafter, Anderson was fired. He then sued the city, claiming his dismissal was a violation of his constitutional rights — and, like Johnson, he lost. The *Anderson* court concluded that the LaVergne Police Department's interest in avoiding sexual harassment suits was a legitimate government interest and that the decision to fire Anderson was constitutional.

Seegmiller and *Anderson* highlight the continuing regulation and punishment of non-marital sex. They also show that marriage remains an effective defense. In both cases, marriage would have negated the state's alleged concerns regarding the employees' sexual relationships. Unfortunately, such protection is not always desirable. While marriage protects the private sexual conduct of consenting adults like Johnson and Anderson, it can also shield employees actively engaging in sexual harassment. This problem has been particularly acute in cases involving same-sex sexual harassment. In these cases, courts have frequently dismissed claims when the alleged harasser was part of a heterosexual marriage. The courts' reasoning in these cases is twofold. First, they appear to hold the false assumption that a person involved in a cross-sex marriage could never harbor same-sex desire, and second, they worry that a finding of same-sex sexual harassment would harm the harasser's marriage. The 2010 case *Smith v. Hy-Vee Inc.* is typical.

Dru Smith, a female employee of a Hy-Vee grocery store, brought a sexual harassment suit against her colleague Sherri Lynch. Smith described a number of incidents that she claimed constituted sexual harassment. The first occurred after Smith observed Lynch "dry humping" a male Hy-Vee manager. After the manager left, Smith said, "God, Sherri, it's like you practically raped him." Lynch replied, "No Dani, if I were going to rape someone, it would be like this." Lynch then pushed Smith up against a wall and held her there while rubbing her hands and body up against Smith. Smith also described a different incident in which Lynch "rubbed her fingers against Smith's fingers and told Smith '[t]hat's what a penis feels like.'" Smith testified that throughout her employment, Lynch repeatedly made sexually suggestive remarks and that she had "smacked [Smith] on the buttocks approximately six times." Lynch had repeatedly fondled and groped Smith, but the court denied the sexual harassment claim because it held Lynch's conduct was not "motivated by a particular attraction to Smith." In reaching its decision, the court emphasized that Lynch has "been married to the same man for sixteen years and [had] two daughters." The court appears to have been influenced by both Smith's heterosexual marriage and a reluctance to upend the lives of her husband and children.

Hy-Vee was not unique. That same year, the Nevada Court of Appeals issued a similar decision in *Sillars v. Nevada*. *Sillars* involved a same-sex sexual harassment claim against a female state employee named Patsy Cave. The plaintiff, Elizabeth Sillars, had been training Cave, and the two struck up a friendship. One night, Cave visited Sillars's house and while drinking, confessed she "had feelings for someone in the office." Sillars named several male employees, and Cave began to cry. A few days later, "Cave called Plaintiff in tears stating, 'I don't want you to think bad of me.' She then asked if she could come to Plaintiff's home and talk to her, but Plaintiff said, 'No, it's late at night.'" After this incident, Sillars noticed that Cave would often stand too close to her and that she would stare at her breasts. At trial, Cave denied having feelings for Sillars, and the court accepted this denial, citing Cave's marriage as proof. According to the court, there is "no evidence demonstrating that Cave is homosexual. Instead, Cave is married and has several children. There is no evidence that she has ever been in, or intends to be in, a homosexual relationship, and Cave denies having romantic feelings for Plaintiff." Sillars's sexual harassment claim was dismissed.

One of the most shocking examples of the marriage defense in a same-sex sexual harassment decision is the 2004 Louisiana case *Kreamer v. Henry's Marine*. In *Kreamer*, the plaintiff, Thomas Kreamer, a deckhand, alleged harassment by his male co-worker, Carroll Carrere. Kreamer testified that Carrere grabbed him by the crotch on eight occasions and that on one of these occasions, Carrere told Kreamer that "he would like to compare packages." Other incidents cited by Kreamer included Carrere blowing kisses at him, putting a hot Zippo lighter between his legs, and staring at him while he slept. Regarding the sleeping incident, Kreamer testified that he woke one morning to find Carrere standing next to his bed just looking at him. When he told Carrere to "get the hell out," Carrere left without saying a word. When Kreamer saw him later, Carrere whistled at him and made "offensive gestures." Kreamer also described an event that occurred toward the end of his employment. According to Kreamer, "Carrere approached [him] from behind as he was bent slightly over the engines, grabbed his sides and said he 'would like to f**k that piece of ass.'" Despite all this testimony, the court denied Kreamer's sexual harassment claim. It concluded that this evidence, "as a whole, reveals an intent of Carrere to humiliate plaintiff for reasons unrelated to a sexual interest, rather than an actual intent to have sexual contact." The court then cited Carrere's heterosexual marriage as proof that Carrere could not have sexually desired Kreamer.

Sexual harassment claims no longer require a finding of desire. In 2020, the US Supreme Court decided *Bostock v.*

Clayton County and held that terminating an employee because of their sexual orientation, or perceived sexual orientation, is a form of sex discrimination. *Bostock*, combined with the court's earlier decision in *Oncale v. Sundowner* (finding that same-sex sexual harassment claims can be actionable), suggests a same-sex harassment case does not require the harasser to be attracted to the victim but can be based solely on the victim's sexual orientation. As a result, *Bostock* may lessen the importance of the marriage defense in same-sex harassment cases, or it may not. None of the above cases included allegations that the victim was harassed because of their sexual orientation. Rather, all involved allegations of explicit desire that were undermined by the defendants' heterosexual marriages.

Marriage and Domestic Violence

In the same-sex sexual harassment cases, marriage provides a problematic yet often effective defense. In the criminal context, the harms of this defense are even more pronounced. Nevertheless, states remain reluctant to eliminate or even limit it. In Arizona, it took the gruesome murder of Penny Williams to convince the legislature that the marital testimonial privilege should only apply to post-marital acts. Many states have not taken even this minimal step.

The Williams case began the morning of November 29, 1978, when the body of Penny Williams was found in the front seat of her automobile near Pantano Wash in Tucson, Arizona. Penny had been stabbed multiple times in the head and neck. The words THE BITCH were printed in dust on the side of the car. Three weeks later, the police received a call from Rita Sipler, the girlfriend of Penny's ex-husband, Scott Williams. Sipler told the police that

Williams had confessed to murdering Penny, and based on this information, Williams was arrested. Sipler was the state's chief witness. However, shortly before the trial commenced, Williams married Sipler. He then asserted the marital testimonial privilege to prevent her from taking the stand. Although the court granted Williams's request, it criticized the privilege, writing, "If it is, perhaps, overly sentimental to wish that marriage should be made in heaven, it is foolish to encourage it to be made on the courthouse steps." The Arizona legislature agreed. Two years later, it limited the privilege to acts occurring after marriage. Other states still do not have such limitations.

In the 2017 Georgia case *U.S. v Davis*, the court confirmed the privilege's continuing applicability to premarital acts. *Davis* involved the prosecution of Joshua Davis, a Brinks armored truck driver and ATM technician. On October 15, 2015, while Davis and his colleague were servicing ATM machines, Davis stole hundreds of thousands of dollars. Davis's colleague did not know of the thefts, and when their truck ran out of gas at the end of their shift, he agreed to stay with the truck and wait for the tow. Davis thanked him and called his girlfriend, Philicia Morris, to pick him up. Then, shortly after Davis left with Morris, his partner called to tell him the police were at the truck and that they were looking for a black bag with money in it. Overhearing this exchange, Morris confronted Davis, asking, "What money, what are you talking about . . . you got money on you or something?" Later, when speaking with the police, Morris told them Davis had answered "yes." She then explained she "freaked out" and "told him to . . . just get it out of [her] car." Davis stuffed the stolen money into a pink bag he found in her car and "threw it out" the car window. Morris then drove Davis back to the Brinks truck where the police were waiting. Later that day, she gave a statement to the FBI, and based on this testimony, Davis was arrested. Shortly thereafter, Davis married Morris and invoked the marital testimonial privilege. Although the government objected, the court upheld the privilege, declaring it vital to protecting "the harmony and sanctity of marriage." The court wrote that there is a *"natural repugnance* in every fair-minded person to compelling a wife or husband to be the means of the other's condemnation, and to compelling the culprit to the humiliation of being condemned by the words of his intimate life partner."

The *Davis* court believed the testimonial privilege fostered marital harmony, but case law shows it is more likely to perpetuate marital violence. Domestic violence exceptions to the testimonial privilege are now universal, specifically because domestic abusers routinely asserted this privilege to avoid prosecution. Unfortunately, even with these exceptions, the spousal testimonial privilege may still be fostering domestic violence. Consider the 2020 Indiana case *U. S. v. Schambers.*

Kenneth Schambers was a convicted felon rearrested for parole violations. While in prison, Schambers sought permission to marry his girlfriend. Permitting the marriage would lead to the exclusion of the girlfriend's testimony, yet the court still granted the request. According to the court, the "concern that the Defendant's request will result in a key witness invoking the adverse spousal testimonial privilege is not enough" to justify infringing his constitutional right to marry. The court then discussed this marital right at length but made only a passing reference to the fact that "among other violations" the defendant was also charged with "Domestic Battery." While details in the opinion are sparse, it appears clear that Schambers was a violent man who would not have hesitated to use threats to obtain his girlfriend's marital consent.

Advocates for victims of domestic abuse note that the testimonial privilege creates a strong incentive for criminal defendants to force — through physical violence or emotional abuse — an unwilling partner to marry them. Dorothy J. Lennig, director of the legal clinic at House of Ruth (a domestic violence shelter in Maryland), testified before the Maryland legislature that coercive marriages are common among abusive men. She noted, "We at the House of Ruth have had multiple clients where their abusers have intimidated them, leaned on them, scared them, forced them into getting married before the trial so they would invoke their spousal privilege." It is therefore ironic that courts continue to uphold the testimonial privilege as respecting the sanctity of marriage and fostering marital harmony.

The testimonial privilege is not the only way marriage continues to benefit abusers. Judicial protection orders offer another example. These protection orders prevent individuals from engaging in violent or threatening acts, harassment, contact, communication, or being in physical proximity to another person. Between 1970 and 1993, most states enacted special laws and proceedings relating to domestic violence protection orders, and they quickly became the most widely used legal remedy against domestic violence. Nevertheless, throughout the 1990s, many courts refused to grant domestic protection orders in the name of marital harmony. At one such hearing, the judge began the proceedings with the comment, "Well, well, well, we had a little domestic squabble, did we? Naughty, naughty. Let's kiss and make up and get out of my court." In another case, the petitioner testified that her husband had repeatedly punched her in the face and presented photographs of her injuries. The judge still denied the protection order, stating:

I am authorized to award you a civil protection order, which could order him to stay away from you and stop hurting you. But I'm not going to do that today.

Because you have children together, you're going to have to find some way to cooperate with each other to raise them. So, I want you to go home and try to work things out in private. And I suggest that you go see a movie I saw recently, called "Mrs. Doubtfire," where Robin Williams and his wife decide to separate, but still manage to find a creative way to work together when it came to their children.

Studies on domestic violence from this period confirm that married abusers routinely received lesser penalties than unmarried abusers. The 1992 DC Gender Bias Task Force Report noted that 70 percent of respondents received shorter sentences in criminal prosecutions where perpetrator and victim were married as compared with violence between strangers. This report also showed that married perpetrators were significantly more likely to receive lighter sentences than those who committed domestic violence outside of the marital relationship. A 1993 report compiled by the Missouri Gender Bias Task Force demonstrated a similar prejudice. This report revealed that judges imposed lighter sentences on defendants convicted of domestic violence crimes than those convicted of assaulting non-intimate-partner strangers and that the greatest reduction was for married perpetrators.

Today, judges, police, and even victims' friends and family remain reluctant to punish marital violence as harshly as non-marital abuse. In her 2021 article, "The Role of Place and Sociodemographic Characteristics on the Issuance of Temporary Civil Protection Orders," sociologist Anne Groggel found that "judges are more likely to issue temporary orders for unmarried victims who cohabit with their abusers than married victims." Groggel blames this difference on a continuing concern for marital harmony, writing that "judges seek to preserve existing marriages and are therefore more reluctant to grant protection orders for married victims than their unmarried counterparts, even after accounting for the recency and severity of abuse."

Sentencing decisions also continue to be influenced by marital status. The 2004 Canadian study "Sentencing Outcomes: A Comparison of Family Violence and Non-Family Violence Cases" found that offenders convicted of violence against their spouse were significantly less likely to receive prison sentences than non-married offenders. It also showed that estranged male spouses were more likely to be imprisoned for domestic violence than current spouses. Moreover, this differential treatment is not limited to legal actors. In their 2005 study on community-based domestic violence norms, sociologists Catherine Taylor and Susan Sorenson showed that non-married domestic violence victims received greater support than married victims for leaving the relationship and for seeking legal interventions. Married victims were likely to be counseled to "try and work things out."

The Marital Rape Exception

The differential treatment of married and unmarried violence is particularly stark with respect to sexual assault. Until the 1990s, most states refused to treat marital rape as a crime and justified this decision with appeals to marital harmony. In the 1981 marital rape case *People v. Brown*, the Supreme Court of Colorado exemplified this view when it wrote that the marital rape exception was beneficial, because it "may remove a substantial obstacle to the resumption of normal marital relations" and "encourag[e] the preservation of family relationships." The 1984 Virginia case *Kizer v. Commonwealth* made similar appeals to marital harmony while also exposing the hollowness of this justification.

Edward and Jeri Kizer were a married couple who had been having marital difficulties for many months. After various attempts at reconciliation, Edward finally moved out. A few weeks later, he met with a friend, and the two discussed "the rape laws of Virginia." Specifically, they discussed the marital rape exception. The friend testified that Edward said, "He was kind of hard up for sex" and that, because he knew he could not be prosecuted, he thought he "ought to go over there and rip [the wife's] clothes off her and take it." The next day, that is what Edward did. He went to Jeri's home, forced his way inside, and raped her in front of their young child. Edward was then convicted of rape, but his conviction was overturned. The appeals court held that it was not clear the "husband perceived, or reasonably should have perceived, that the marriage actually was ended." Consequently, Edward could not be convicted of rape.

Marriage is no longer an absolute defense to rape, yet it continues to provide significant protections. In many states, the bar for prosecuting sexually abusive spouses is higher than for non-spouses; proof of additional elements, such as force or resistance, is often required. Other states maintain distinct reporting requirements for spousal rape. These include requiring that victims immediately report marital rape or lose their right to press charges. Marital rape is also, frequently, punished less severely than non-marital rape. In Maryland, until 2023, a spouse could not be charged with first- or second-degree rape, the two most serious charges. In South Carolina, marital rape convictions can receive no more than ten years, while non-marital rapes can receive up to thirty, and in Virginia, when the offender is the spouse of the victim, the judge may suspend a guilty judgment and order counseling "if the court finds such action will promote maintenance of the family unit and be in the best interest of the complaining witness."

The different treatment of marital and non-marital rape is also apparent in cases involving capacity to consent. Many states exempt spouses from prohibitions forbidding sex with a mentally incompetent person. In 2015, the issue of spousal consent and mental competence garnered national attention when seventy-eight-year-old former Iowa legislator Henry Rayhons was charged with rape. Rayhons's wife, Donna, was suffering from Alzheimer's, yet he continued having sex with her even after being informed that she could no longer consent. State prosecutors argued that sex with Donna was rape, but at trial the jury sided with Rayhons. Donna was Rayhons's wife, thus, her inability to consent to sex appears to have been deemed irrelevant.

Heat of Passion

The greater tolerance for marital violence is also apparent in the continuing acceptance of the heat of passion defense. Throughout the 1990s, courts routinely excused marital violence as an understandable and forgivable reaction to marital infidelity. In one 1993 New Hampshire case, an estranged husband violently assaulted his wife after discovering her camping with another man. The husband was convicted of assault but sentenced to only twenty-eight days in prison and permitted to serve this time on the weekends. According to the judge, although the couple had been separated for a year, the victim was still legally the defendant's wife, thus "I can't conclude that [the attack] was completely unprovoked. I think that would provoke the average man." The same year, an Ohio man with a record for murder, rape, and armed robbery entered his estranged wife's home and found her in bed with another man. He beat her with a crowbar and knocked out her daughter's teeth when the girl attempted to call 911. The Ohio court sentenced the man to the state-mandated fifteen years but released him after seven months. The judge explained, "The guy walked into his house with his wife in his bed with another guy. It's enough to blow any guy's cool if he's any kind of man." One year later, in 1994, Kenneth Peacock shot his wife in the head several hours after finding her in bed with another man. Peacock pleaded guilty to voluntary manslaughter, yet the Maryland judge was reluctant to sentence him. The judge likened the case to a drunk driving accident, declaring, "The most difficult thing that a judge is called upon to do . . . is sentencing noncriminals as criminals." The judge added, "I seriously wonder how many married men, married five years or four years would have the strength to walk away, but without inflicting some corporal punishment . . . I shudder to think what I would do."

The idea that a husband should be excused for a violent response to infidelity remains widespread. In nearly all US jurisdictions, a husband who commits violence upon discovering his wife in the act of adultery can receive a mitigated sentence or charge. Marriage remains the key to this defense. Courts are much more likely to find the defense inapplicable when an unmarried man is subject to infidelity. It is a wife's disloyalty, either through actual adultery or sometimes just a desire to leave the marriage, that is treated as uniquely provoking. The 2007 case *People v. Le* is one more recent example.

In Le, Johnny Viet Le killed his wife's lover, Truoung (known as Thang). When Le first discovered the affair, he confronted his wife, Pham, who promised to stop. Despite her promise, the affair continued. When Le learned of the affair again, Pham again promised to end it. When Le discovered for the third time that the affair had not ended, he told Pham he wanted to meet Thang. Pham objected, and Le became very angry. He arranged the meeting without Pham's help (he pretended to be a potential customer) and then butchered Thang with a meat cleaver. Le was arrested and convicted of second-degree murder. On appeal, the conviction was reversed. The California Court of Appeal held that the evidence supported a finding that Le was provoked, and the jury should have received an instruction on voluntary manslaughter.

The *Le* court sympathized with Le and viewed his violence as uncharacteristic and understandable. In describing Le, the court wrote, he is a "47-year-old man with a peaceful disposition and no criminal record." It was his wife who was presented as the real culprit. Pham's insults toward Le on the day of the murder were described "as the spark that caused this powder keg of accumulated provocation to explode." According to the court, this provocation caused Le to act "rashly and under the influence of intense emotion that obscured [his] reasoning or judgment." Consequently, the court held that a manslaughter instruction was appropriate. Notably, in reversing Le's conviction, the court emphasized how much Le loved Pham and how horrible it was for him to discover she "still loved Thang." Le hacked a man to death with a meat cleaver, but because his wife cheated, the court found him sympathetic.

Ironically, while marriage excuses violence and protects abusers, it is often touted as doing the opposite. In their 2014 *Washington Post* article, "The Best Way to End Violence Against Women? Stop Taking Lovers and Get Married," law professors Brad Wilcox and Robin Wilson argued that women can avoid physical and sexual violence by getting married. They noted that married women are victimized less than other women and suggested this statistical difference was because marriage "cause[s] men to behave better." Wilcox and Wilson claimed that married men are less violent than unmarried men because they "tend to settle down after they marry, to be more attentive to the expectations of friends and kin, to be more faithful, and to be more committed to their partners — factors that minimize the risk of violence." The article presented marriage as the cure for male violence, and domestic violence victim advocates were quick to criticize this claim. As one wrote, "The last thing that women in abusive relationships need is to be told that they can turn a bad man good by marrying him."

The freedom to commit abuse is rarely acknowledged as a marriage incentive. One exception is mail-order marriage. In the context of mail-order marriage, the idea that men are marrying to abuse is widely accepted. In 1999, an Immigration and Naturalization Service report on the international mail-order bride industry stated:

> While no national figures exist on abuse of alien wives, there is every reason to believe that the incidence is higher in this population than for the nation as a whole. Authorities agree that abuse in these marriages can be expected based on the men's desire for a submissive wife and the women's desire for a better life.

Organizations such as Tahirih Justice Center, which works to end violence against women, have also suggested that men seek mail-order marriage to perpetuate abuse. Layli Miller-Muro, the executive director of Tahirih Justice Center, stated, "[The mail-order-bride] industry predominantly places women at a disadvantage where the man is the paying client and the woman advertised as a product, a commodity." According to Muro, this creates a "presumption of power and a potentially very dangerous recipe for abuse." In 2005, Congress responded to these fears with the International Marriage Broker Regulation Act (IMBRA). The act accepts the idea that men seek mail-order marriage to perpetuate abuse, and it provides mail-order brides with special rights and protections to reduce that possibility.

Whether mail-order brides are more likely to be abused than other wives is hotly debated. Nevertheless, the discussion surrounding mail-order marriage and abuse shows that, in this context, abuse is recognized as a potential marital motivation. The other obvious example is child marriage. It is now widely assumed that most child marriages are motivated by adult men's desire to legally engage in child sexual abuse. As historian Nicolas Syrett writes in his book *American Child Bride*, "Contemporary observers may recoil when an older man marries a much younger girl . . . because they suspect him of pedophilia." He notes, "Marriage, in this analysis, is simply a back door to that which is illegal outside of it."

Child Marriage

Sex with a child is a strict liability crime. This means the child's "consent" is irrelevant. The well-known adage "sixteen will get you twenty" (meaning sex with a sixteen-year-old will subject you to a twenty-year jail sentence) is a recognition of the strict liability aspect of state statutory rape laws. Still, marriage remains an effective defense, and until relatively recently it was a defense actively promoted by many states. A disturbing 1997 law review article about child marriage in Orange County, California, revealed that a county social service agency routinely advised pregnant teenagers, some as young as thirteen or fourteen, to marry their statutory rapists. According to the article, agency officials promised not to report the fathers of these girls' babies to law enforcement authorities if the parties agreed to marry. Such tactics worked. After being "shaken by threats of arrest," most men agreed to marry the children they had impregnated. The article also revealed that once the threat of jail had passed, many of these men abandoned their child brides.

Today, anti-child-marriage advocates, many who are former child victims themselves, have been slowly changing state child marriage laws. Sherry Johnson is one such advocate. Johnson was eight years old when she was raped by an adult member of her church in the late 1960s. When she became pregnant at ten, the police started an investigation, but the investigation ended when Johnson's parents and the church elders pressured her to marry her rapist. "They took the handcuffs from handcuffing him," she said, referring to the risk he faced of arrest for rape, "to handcuffing me." Eventually, Johnson divorced her rapist and began working to protect other children from sharing a similar fate.

Due to the efforts of advocates like Johnson, states are increasingly restricting child marriages. Some have done so by limiting underage marriage to parties within a similar age range. Florida requires that the spouse of a child bride be no more than two years older than the child, while Arizona sets a three-year age gap. Other states have restricted child marriages by raising the age of consent. Recently, both Virginia and New Jersey have raised the age of consent to eighteen. These changes are encouraging, but they are not universal. Many states continue to permit underage marriage and allow child sexual abusers to avoid prosecution. In addition, the problem of underage marriages may soon become worse. In 2022, the US Supreme Court eliminated the constitutional right to abortion. Shortly thereafter, many states began banning access to abortion. Without abortion, there will be fewer options to hide the evidence of child sex crimes. This may become an increasingly powerful reason to marry, but it also underscores the deep-seated problems with the marriage defense.

When most women were at the financial and sexual mercy of men, the criminal defense benefits of marriage were justifiable. The availability of the marriage defense could force reluctant men into marriage or allow vulnerable women to leave dangerous relationships. However, the connection between marriage and criminal prosecution was always an imperfect solution to women's economic, legal, and sexual vulnerabilities. The defense protected vulnerable women from certain harms but exacerbated others. Today, the positive aspects of the marriage defense have largely disappeared. Its primary benefits are for those wishing to abuse, and, sadly, many still marry for these protections.

chapter five

The Married Parent

Maternity is a matter of fact. Paternity is a matter of opinion.

— AMERICAN PROVERB

Shortly after the conclusion of World War I, a young English-woman, known as E.A., arrived at Ellis Island with her three-month-old baby. As a single woman with a child, E.A. was detained by immigration officials as potentially "immoral." Then, after a hearing before a board of special inquiry, she was ordered deported. Just before E.A. was removed, Mrs. C.B. of Baltimore, the wife of the baby's father, intervened and filed an appeal. Mrs. C.B had sent E.A. the money to travel to the United States, and she testified that she and her husband wished to adopt the child. She also noted that she was fully aware the baby was the result of an affair between Mr. C.B. and E.A. that occurred while he was serving with the US armed forces in England. Despite the affair, Mrs. C.B. defended E.A.'s virtue. She described E.A. as "far removed from the deadline of immorality laid down by the immigration laws" and pronounced her "a lovable, refined girl." In further defense of E.A.'s morality, Mrs. C.B. noted that her brother-in-law, G.B., was willing to marry her. In a separate affidavit, G.B. confirmed Mrs. C.B.'s claim, writing, "I am perfectly willing to marry [E.A.] and be her faithful husband as long as I live for I know that her moral character is good." Mrs. C.B. concluded her plea to the immigration authorities by averring that she strongly supported a marriage between E.A. and G.B. and that it "would never disturb her happiness with her husband."

The *New York Times* article on the E.A./C.B love triangle —
"Romance of War Puzzles Officials" — presented the story as
baffling. Yet C.B.'s actions were perfectly rational given America's
harsh immigration laws and non-marital fathers' limited parental rights. C.B. cheated on his wife while stationed abroad. His
girlfriend, E.A., became pregnant, but because C.B. was married,
he could not marry E.A. More important, because he was not
married to E.A., C.B. had no rights to the child. To gain rights
to his son, C.B. needed to adopt him. He also needed E.A. to
agree, but it appears E.A. would only agree to the adoption if
she remained part of her son's life. Therefore, the question was
how to bring both E.A. and the child to America. As an unwed
mother, E.A. fell afoul of the immoral purposes provision of the
1907 Immigration Act. The C.B.s solved this problem by having
C.B.'s brother agree to marry E.A.

The specific situation of the C.B.'s was rare, but the custody
problems facing non-marital fathers like C.B. were common.
Historically, paternal rights were established through marriage,
and men had no rights to the children they fathered outside of
wedlock. Thus, American custody law proceeded as follows: "The
mother is the woman who bears the child, and the father is the
husband of the mother." Obviously, this was not always biolog-
ically true, but legally it was correct. As a result, marriage was
crucially important in securing the custodial rights of fathers.

Parental Rights Under the Common Law

Under common law, a man had complete authority over any
children born of his wife. His authority was so absolute that he
could even convey custody of the child to a third person without
the mother's consent and over her objection. Conversely, a man
had no legal relationship to a child he sired out of wedlock. A

non-marital father could not even effectively adopt such a child. The nineteenth-century inheritance case *Safford v. Houghton's Estate* highlights this problem. In *Safford*, the father had a child outside of marriage and then adopted him. The adoption meant the child could inherit from the father, but as the *Safford* court explained, it did not make the child legitimate, and thus it did not make him the legal heir of his biological grandfather. The court held, "To Abel Houghton, the father, and to all other kindred of George F., Frederick remained as before the adoption — an Ishmael — *filius nullius* — base-born, with no heritable quality in his blood."

Although fathers could not legitimate their non-marital children through adoption, they could do so through marriage. This different treatment was intentional. As legal historian Lawrence Friedman explains, "Only 'families' in the traditional sense could have babies. If you wanted sex, you were supposed to get married. If you wanted babies, you were supposed to get married. Sex and babies were otherwise (officially) off limits." Limiting paternal rights to marriage helped facilitate men's willingness to marry. However, this was only one of the parental benefits of marriage. An equally important benefit was the legal presumption that all husbands, regardless of biology, were the fathers of their wives' children.

The marital presumption was a legal fiction created to deal with the fact that, for most of history, men could rarely be certain they were the genetic parent of their children. The presumption had been part of English common law for centuries, but it was only codified in the late eighteenth century as cuckoldry fears increased. By linking marriage to legal fatherhood, the marital presumption ensured men could "guarantee" their paternity and justified the wisdom of assuming responsibility for children that might not be their biological progeny.

In contrast with the robust parental rights of husbands,

The Cuckold Departs for the Hunt. Metal print by Isaac Cruikshank.

the rights of unmarried fathers were almost non-existent. Non-marital children were *filius nullius*, meaning, literally, the "children of no one." Technically, both unmarried fathers and unmarried mothers lacked legal rights to their children, but in practice, only unmarried fathers lacked such rights. The vicious legal battle between Tillatha Catherine Bennett and her gold miner husband Isaac Graham highlights the stark difference between the rights of married and unmarried parents during the first half of the nineteenth century.

In 1845, twenty-one-year-old Tillatha Bennett wed forty-five-year-old Isaac Graham. The relationship quickly turned violent, but by that time Bennett was already pregnant and could not leave without forfeiting custody of her child. Bennet remained with Graham for five years. Then, one day, a young man arrived at the homestead. The man was Graham's son from his first marriage, and he revealed that his mother was still very much alive. The Graham-Bennett marriage was bigamous. This meant Bennett was an unmarried mother and, under the law, the sole

Issac Graham.

legal custodian of her children. Shortly thereafter, Bennett fled with her two children (and most of Graham's gold). Eventually, Graham tracked her down and took the children back to California. Bennett then followed and sued for custody.

Initially, Bennett did not raise the bigamy defense (presumably she was reluctant to officially declare her children bastards). Instead, she claimed her actions were justified by Graham's cruelty. She published a letter in a San Francisco newspaper detailing Graham's abuse and wrote she had fled because she was "so tired of being beat and having Bowie knives drawn over me . . . for twice that old brute Graham drew his Bowie knife across my throat until blood ran down my breast and I expected every day he would kill me." The abuse Bennett suffered was horrendous, but it did not entitle her to custody. Eventually, with no other option, Bennett argued that Graham lacked paternity rights because their marriage was bigamous.

Initially, Bennett's bigamy argument was successful. The lower court agreed that because Graham's first wife was alive when Bennett and Graham married, their marriage was void. Bennett was granted sole custody of the children, and Graham appealed. The California Supreme Court then reversed the lower court's decision, holding that despite Graham's living first wife, his marriage to Bennett was valid. The court defended its dubious legal decision, claiming it was unwilling to condemn the children to bastardy. However, the real reason may have been less altruistic.

Graham was a violent man. Only a few years earlier, he had led a successful coup against the Mexican governor of Northern California and then planned a second insurrection against his replacement. Graham's son was similarly violent. After Bennett fled with the children, he shot at her mother and then murdered her brother. The court had good reason to worry about angering Graham. This may be why, despite the parents' obviously bigamous marriage, the court declared the Graham-Bennett children legitimate. Then, once it did so, all other factors, including Graham's violence and abuse, became irrelevant. As the legal father, Graham was entitled to custody.

The rule that a husband's parental rights were absolute derived from the 1804 English case *Rex v. De Manneville*. In *De Manneville* the court gave custody of a nursing infant to its father despite the uncontested claim that the mother had only separated from the father to escape his horrendous abuse. The court also ignored the fact that De Manneville was a convicted criminal and Jacobite traitor and had broken into the mother's family home, literally grabbed the infant from her breast, and fled with it into a terrible storm. All that mattered was marriage. Because De Manneville had married the mother, he had the right to the child. As Lord Eldon, the lord chancellor deciding *De Manneville*, stated, "The law is clear that the custody of a child, of whatever age, belongs to the father [and] the father's rights extend to the hour of a child's birth."

American courts cited *De Manneville* for the proposition that married fathers should always receive custody of their children. Still, they were often more open to considering parental conduct than their English peers. In his 1884 *Commentaries on Equity Jurisprudence*, Supreme Court justice Joseph Story notes the presumptive authority of the married father to custody, but also suggests limitations:

> For although in general parents are entrusted with the custody of the persons and the education of their children, yet this is done upon the natural presumption that the children will be properly taken care of, and will be brought up with a due education in literature and morals and religion, and that they will be treated with kindness and affection. But whenever this presumption is removed, whenever (for example) it is found that a father is guilty of gross ill-treatment or cruelty towards his infant children; or that he is in constant habits of drunkenness and blasphemy, or low and gross debauchery; or that he professes atheistical or irreligious principles; or that his domestic associations are such as tend to the corruption and contamination of his children; or that he otherwise acts in a manner injurious to the morals or interests of his children, — in every such case the Court of Chancery will interfere and deprive him of the custody of his children, and appoint a suitable person to act as guardian and to take care of them and to superintend their education.

As Story notes, American courts presumed paternal custody but would consider giving custody to a more suitable person, if justified by the circumstances. Typically, this meant the child's mother.

The Rise of Maternal Rights

The idea of giving custody of children to mothers, not fathers, was supported by the nineteenth century's separate-spheres ideology. Often termed the cult of domesticity, these beliefs identified women with the home and family and supported the idea that maternal instincts made women the natural custodians of young children. The highly publicized 1840 Pennsylvania custody case *D'Hauteville v. Sears* was the first to argue for a maternal preference. The case involved a custody dispute between Ellen Sears, the daughter of a wealthy Boston merchant, and the Baron Gonzalve D'Hauteville, a Swiss nobleman. The couple met and married in Europe, but the relationship quickly deteriorated. Sears didn't like living in Switzerland and considered her husband a bully and a tyrant. D'Hauteville was similarly unhappy. He thought his wife was too independent-minded and neglected her wifely duties. He also didn't like the fact that his mother-in-law had been living with the couple since the wedding. Sears became pregnant, but by the time she returned to the US to give birth, the two were barely speaking. After the baby was born, she decided to stay.

As a married mother, especially one who had deserted her husband, Sears did not have the law on her side. The law presumed a marital child belonged to the father. Therefore, Sears's only option was to challenge this presumption. Sears claimed custody decisions should be based on the parents' relationship to the child, not marriage. She also argued that young children, in particular, needed the special care only a mother could provide. Surprisingly, the court agreed. According to the court, "Everyone knows that a father is unfit to care for an infant; physically unfit and unfit by reason of his avocations." It then declared, "No substitute can supply the place of [a mother]." Consequently, against all odds, Sears won.

Family Prayer, circa 1871, by Currier and Ives.

As the nineteenth century progressed, women were increasingly considered the preferred caretakers of young children, and only deeply unwomanly behavior, usually related to accusations of immorality, could overcome the maternal preference. In the 1854 case *Lindsey v. Lindsey*, the Georgia Supreme Court explained this morality exception and why it defeated the maternal presumption. In *Lindsey*, the court refused to give custody of a child to an adulterous mother despite recognizing the woman had only left her husband after suffering terrible abuse. The court wrote, "In the eye of an omniscient God, the weak and erring woman may not be, (to say the least,) the more sinful and degraded of the two. But . . . in the opinion of society, it is otherwise." According to the court, having violated the marriage contract, an adulterous wife inevitably found herself reduced to "utter and irredeemable ruin, where her associations are with the vulgar, the vile and the depraved. If her children be with her, their characters must be, more or less, influenced and harmed by the circumstances which surround them." As a result, even if her actions were justified, an adulterous mother still could not be given custody of her children.

Barring immorality, women became the favored custodians of children, and this maternal preference even included unmarried women. By the late nineteenth century, adoption by single women, many of whom had lost fiancés and sweethearts during the Civil War, became accepted and encouraged. "Leftover women" and "leftover children" were considered the perfect match. In 1912, *Harper's Bazaar* exemplified this view when it published a glowing profile of Mary Hildreth, an unmarried, adoptive mother of ten children living in New Hampshire. Hildreth adopted her first child in the late 1880s after a friend, "to whom she was deeply attached," married and had a child. According to the article, Hildreth fell in love with her friend's new baby and decided that "she could not endure to be without a possession so wonderful and desirable." She then adopted a child about the same age and, as the article noted, "the two women — one married, one not — spent the next few years comparing infant accomplishments." The story ended by noting that Hildreth "could not love the children more if they were her own."

As unmarried adoption became acceptable, some social reformers began advocating for the elimination of distinctions between marital and non-marital families more generally. These reformers recognized that such differences harmed children, especially laws related to illegitimacy. Reformers contended that "there may be illegitimate parents, but there can be no illegitimate children." In 1920, two regional conferences were organized by the Children's Bureau and the Inter-city Conference on Illegitimacy to consider ways to eliminate the distinctions between marital and non-marital families. One proposal was the Uniform Illegitimacy Act. This act would have entitled unmarried children to parental support, but it never gained widespread support.

Although some child welfare advocates sought to reform illegitimacy laws, others were highly resistant. Despite acknowledging the problems with marriage-based parental rights and obligations, these men and women believed that such changes could not be made without undermining the marital family. In 1919, Bradley Hull, a social justice reformer and an attorney with the Cleveland Humane Society, exemplified such views when he argued against illegitimacy reform, warning, "If you put the illegitimate child on a basis of equality with the child born of the man wedded wife, there is a great source of danger." According to Hull, the question was whether "the child or the home [is] to be the unit of the state? If you're going to make, as far as the economic basis is concerned, the status of the unmarried mother and her child equal to that of the married woman and her child, you're going to do something to unsettle society." A few years later, child welfare advocate Emma O. Lundberg made a similar assessment. She declared, "In practically all states, up to the present time, it has been held incompatible with the interest of the legal family to place the child of illegitimate birth upon and equally with the children born in wedlock."

Reforming Illegitimacy Laws

As attempts to reform state illegitimacy laws failed, support for the marital family grew, and even the prior approval of single-parent adoption began to wane. In the 1920s and '30s, motherhood was still viewed as women's primary role. However, as adoption historian Julie Berebitsky notes, "Now it was understood as part of the experience of the sexually satisfied and emotionally fulfilled wife." Single women were increasingly viewed as abnormal and potentially sexually deviant, and child welfare experts began arguing that these women

should not be allowed to adopt. By 1945, child welfare workers attending the National Conference of Social Work openly
described "unmarried people" as "obviously disqualified [from
adopting]" and grouped them with the "mentally ill" and "alco-
holics." It was not until the late 1960s that the different treatment of marital families and non-marital families was finally,
seriously, questioned.

In 1968, the US Supreme Court decided *Levy v. Louisiana.*
Levy was a wrongful death suit brought by five non-marital children after the death of their mother by her doctor's alleged negli-
gence. The lower court rejected the children's claim, holding that
the state statute only applied to a "legitimate child." On appeal,
the Supreme Court reversed. The court held that the children's
illegitimacy had no rational relation to the wrong inflicted on
the mother, and thus the statute violated the Equal Protection
Clause of the Fourteenth Amendment. The *Levy* court also
forcefully rejected the doctrine of *filius nullius* and the idea
that illegitimate children are "non-persons." As Justice Douglas
poignantly noted, "They are humans, live, and have their being,"
therefore they are entitled to equal protection under the law.

Shortly after deciding *Levy*, the court decided *Glona v.
American Guarantee. Glona* was another wrongful death case,
but this one was brought by a mother for the wrongful death of
her non-marital son. The lower court held that because Glona's
son was born out of wedlock, she had no right to bring an action
for his death. The Supreme Court reversed and once again held
there was no justifiable basis for the distinction between marital
and non-marital children.

Levy and *Glona* were limited to the role of illegitimacy in
the wrongful death context, but four years later, in *Stanley v.
Illinois*, the Supreme Court expanded on these rulings when
it struck down a state law forbidding unmarried fathers from
receiving custody. *Stanley* concerned the parental rights of Peter

Stanley, an unmarried father who had lived, off and on, with his girlfriend, Joan Stanley, and their three children for eighteen years. When Joan died, Stanley sought custody of their children. However, because he had never married Joan, Illinois refused to recognize him as a legal parent. Stanley was denied custody, and his children became wards of the state. Stanley then challenged the constitutionality of the Illinois custody law and won.

Stanley v. Illinois was a major victory for the rights of unmarried fathers, but it was not a rejection of the long-standing connection between marriage and parenthood. Despite ruling for Stanley, the court largely agreed with the state's argument that "the presence or absence of the father from the home on a day-to-day basis and the responsibility imposed upon the relationship" typically distinguished married fathers from unmarried fathers and justified giving them greater rights. The *Stanley* court simply held that in the rare case that an unmarried father behaved like a married father — living with and caring for his children — then such a man could also be entitled to parental rights. The court did not find that married and unmarried fathers needed to be treated equally.

Five years later, the Supreme Court decided *Quilloin v. Walcott* and confirmed that when determining parental rights, marriage still trumped biology. *Quilloin* concerned an unmarried father's objection to his child's adoption by the mother's new husband. The trial court denied Quilloin's request to prevent the adoption, and on appeal the Supreme Court affirmed this decision. *Quilloin* described the unmarried father in *Stanley* as the exception and held that marriage, not biology, remained the primary means of conferring paternal rights. Quilloin, unlike Stanley, had not behaved like a married father. He had not lived with his child or the mother. Therefore, the court held it was not discriminatory to distinguish an unmarried father like Quilloin from marital fathers. Unmarried fathers could possess parental rights, but in most cases the rights of married fathers remained greater.

Marriage and Contraceptives

The Supreme Court's 1965 decision in *Griswold v. Connecticut* also highlighted the connection between marriage and parental rights. In *Griswold*, the court held that married people, but not single people, had the right to use contraceptives and thus, control the decision to become a parent. This victory was the culmination of a decades-long campaign to legalize contraceptives for married couples.

One of the earliest marriage-based contraceptive arguments was made in 1918 by family planning pioneer Marie Stopes in her controversial book *Married Love*. Stopes's book intentionally focused on married couples. Both the explicitly marriage-focused title, and the opening sentence — "Every heart desires a mate" — set the book's marital tone. By linking contraceptives to marriage, Stopes redefined this taboo subject as acceptable and necessary — at least for married couples. She even suggests that her own marriage might have been saved if she had possessed greater sexual knowledge. "In my own marriage I paid such a terrible price for sex-ignorance that I feel that knowledge gained at such cost should be placed at the service of humanity."

Less than a decade after *Married Love* was published, Margaret Sanger released her similarly groundbreaking book *Happiness in Marriage*. Like Stopes, Sanger focused on contraceptive use by married couples and specifically argued that birth control was essential to creating strong and healthy marriages. Together, Stopes and Sanger helped change the public's perception of marital contraceptive use. By the 1930s, polls showed that

MARRIED LOVE
By Dr. MARIE STOPES.
Price 6/6, post free, from:
HEALTH PROMOTION Ltd.,
186, Efficiency House, Paternoster Sq., E.C.4

most Americans supported marital birth control. In 1965, birth control advocates used this long-standing support for marital contraception to successfully challenge the constitutionality of Connecticut's contraceptive ban.

Griswold involved a state ban on contraceptive use. The state defended the law, arguing that it helped deter promiscuity and other forms of sexual immorality. The *Griswold* court disagreed. The court found these arguments could justify a prohibition on contraceptive use outside of marriage but were inapplicable to married couples. It held that contraceptive use was different within marriage. When spouses used contraceptives, they were transformed into something moral, appropriate, and constitutionally protected.

Griswold established a constitutional right to contraceptive use for married couples, and shortly thereafter, in *Eisenstadt v. Baird*, the court extended this right to unmarried partners. *Eisenstadt* eliminated *Griswold*'s marital requirement. However, the case did not portend a rejection of the marital preference more generally. Eisenstadt could have cast doubt on the use of marriage as a criterion for numerous other parental rights and benefits, but it did not. As law professor Susan Frelich Appleton has written, "Despite *Eisenstadt*'s promise to make marriage irrelevant for important decisions in intimate life, marriage has persisted as the holy grail in family law."

Marriage and Parental Rights Today

One of the most famous modern examples of marrying for parental rights was the 1996 marriage of Michael Jackson and Debbie Rowe. Initially, the public didn't know what to make of the Jackson-Rowe marriage, and their union was largely greeted with confusion. Unlike Jackson's earlier marriage to Lisa Marie Presley — a lavish affair and very public — the Jackson-Rowe marriage was secretive. Jackson didn't even confirm the marriage until months later. Nevertheless, when considering the very different purpose of this marriage, Jackson's behavior makes sense. Jackson married Rowe to become a father, and years later Rowe confirmed that the couple only wed after she offered her womb as a "gift."

Jackson was wealthy and famous. Undoubtedly there were other ways he could have become a parent. Still, marrying Rowe was probably the most effective. Marriage is the only legally binding agreement guaranteeing a man's parental rights before birth. Any non-marital parenting agreement with Rowe (or any other woman who agreed to bear his child) would have been risky. Adoption would also have been difficult given Jackson's scandal-plagued history; even surrogacy could have been problematic if Jackson was not (as is frequently suggested) genetically related to his children. Marriage solved all these problems. Upon marriage, Jackson became the presumed father of Rowe's children, and once she gave birth, no additional steps were needed for him to assume legal and physical custody. Moreover, by marrying Rowe, any doubts surrounding her children's genetic paternity became legally irrelevant. Jackson was the father.

Historically, the marital presumption benefited husbands, like Jackson, men who may or may not have been the biological fathers of their spouses' children. At a time when paternity could rarely be proved, this presumption made sense. However, paternity tests are now highly accurate. Consequently, the presumption is no longer about providing a practical solution to the question of paternity. Rather, its continuation is an intentional choice to elevate the rights of marital fathers over non-marital fathers. Notably, in the 1988 Supreme Court case *Michael H. v. Gerald R.*, the court had the opportunity to eliminate the marital presumption — and it declined.

Michael H. involved a love triangle. Carol, who was married to Gerald, had an affair with Michael and became pregnant. After waffling back and forth between the two men, Carol ultimately chose to raise the child with Gerald. Michael then sought custodial rights, and the court refused his request. Despite recognizing that Michael was almost certainly the biological father (genetic testing was still relatively new), the court protected Gerald's paternity rights. According to the court, the purpose of the marital presumption was to safeguard marriage and marital harmony. The court held that the invention of accurate paternity testing did not undermine the marital presumption. Marriage trumped biology.

The marital presumption has weakened since *Michael H.*, but it remains a significant benefit of marriage. In most states, rebutting the presumption is extremely difficult. Even if a man obtains a DNA test indicating he is a child's biological father, it doesn't mean he has the right to present this evidence to the court. At least six states have statutes denying genetic fathers' standing to challenge the paternity of a marital child. Moreover, even in states where such challenges are permissible, a court can refuse to allow a paternity challenge if it determines it would not be in the child's best interest. In addition, even if a court permits a paternity challenge and hears DNA evidence, it can still determine that it is in the child's best interest for the husband to maintain his status as the legal father.

A 2015 study on the use of marriage as a "risk reduction

strategy" showed that men are aware of marriage's parenthood benefits and that they will marry for them. Many of the study's male participants "felt that taking advantage of [legal] benefits is a legitimate reason to marry, particularly when expecting a child." These men cited securing paternity rights as "the big advantage of marrying." Notably, the most highly educated male participants were especially cognizant of the fact that "marriage was the best way to secure parental rights." One man noted that he and his partner had initially planned to enter into a registered partnership because they didn't want "the fuss" of marriage. "But then we started to look closely at all the arrangements and yes, marriage is a good institution. Everything is covered at once and everything is cared for."

The study also revealed that the more paternity motivates men's marital decisions, the more men are willing to "pay" women for mating opportunities. Notably, the men least able to offer attractive compensation to potential wives were also the most disapproving of marrying for parental rights. These less-well-off participants described marrying for parenthood as too strategic and complained that people in such marriages were not marrying for the right reasons. As one participant noted, "When you are expecting a child you shouldn't get married because of the mere fact that marriage is securing your rights, because then you are only marrying for the child, and not because you yourself are ready."

Single Status and Moral Fitness

Single men are not the only ones who marry for parental rights. Marriage can also play an important role in divorced parents' custody disputes, especially when there are accusations of immorality. In the past, arguing that a mother was morally unfit was one of the few ways a father could successfully challenge the maternal custody presumption. Today, such accusations (often involving unmarried cohabitation) continue to provide fathers with one of the most effective tools for gaining custody.

Cohabiting parents are often dismayed to find they have few defenses against charges of immorality. For example, in the 1990 Michigan case *Helms v. Helms*, a mother lost custody of her children due to her unmarried cohabitation despite prior case law holding that unmarried cohabitation did not constitute immorality. The *Helms* court simply distinguished the prior cases based on the fact that the mother in *Helms* was cohabitating *and* pregnant. The court held that this difference made the prior cohabitation cases inapplicable and then awarded custody of the children to the father. Similarly, in the 2000 case *Ulvund v. Ulvund* an unmarried mother was living with her same-sex partner, and due to same-sex marriage bans, the couple could not marry. Therefore, to avoid possible accusations of immorality, the mother refrained from all displays of affection toward her partner in front of the child. Unfortunately, not only were such precautions ineffective, they were also actually detrimental. In considering the father's change in custody petition, the *Ulvund* court held that the mother's lack of affection toward her partner was unnatural and harmful. It then placed the child with the father, noting, "He and his wife do express affection for each other in their home."

More recent cases confirm the continuing difficulties facing unmarried parents in cohabiting relationships. In the 2010 Mississippi case *Brumfield v. Brumfield*, the state appellate court held that the mother's non-marital sexual relationships were relevant to its custody determination while also holding that the father's domestic violence — he had beaten the mother with a belt — was immaterial. According to the court, the father's actions need not be considered because it was "only" a single occurrence. One year later, in *Masters v. Masters*, the Mississippi court again held that non-marital relationships could justify a change in custody. In *Masters*, the non-custodial father sought a change in custody based on the fact that the mother had lived with three different men in the nine years since the couple's divorce. The appellate court agreed that such non-marital cohabitation could warrant a change in custody and remanded the case to the trial court to consider the effects of mother's "unstable marital and extramarital relationships" upon the child's welfare.

Remarrying for Custody

Given the fact that unmarried parents, especially mothers, are vulnerable to accusations of immorality, many have decided that the best way to neutralize this threat is to marry. The 1990 Arkansas case *Holmes v. Holmes* is illustrative. In *Holmes*, the father sought a change in custody based on the fact that the mother "had engaged in extra-marital affairs" while married to her second husband (not him), and that she began cohabitating with another man after her second marriage had ended. The court agreed with the father that the mother's unmarried cohabitation was concerning, and it appeared poised to order a change in custody. Then, recognizing she was about to lose custody, the mother quickly assured the court that she and her boyfriend intended to get married. By the rehearing they were married and the court held there was no longer any reason to order a change in custody. According to the court, the mother's "recent marriage was sufficient to overcome her previous, unstable conduct."

The 2004 Arkansas case *Powell v. Marshall* is similar. In *Powell*, the court noted that the mother "has lived for an extended period of time with a person who was not her husband

[and] continued to cohabit with [this man] after the filing of the Petition for Change of Custody." The trial court then granted a change in custody based on this non-marital cohabitation, and the mother appealed. While the appeal was pending, the mother married her boyfriend. The appellate court then held the mother was "no longer out of compliance with the court orders," and the change in custody decision was reversed.

As non-marital cohabitation has become increasingly common, some parents have challenged the continuing judicial preference for marriage over cohabitation. The 2016 Utah case *Robertson v. Robertson* is one example. In *Robertson*, both the mother and father were in non-marital cohabitating relationships, which the court viewed as extremely concerning. Consequently, once the mother married her boyfriend, she was quickly declared the more "moral parent" and awarded custody. The unmarried father then challenged this custody determination. He argued there has been a "significant shift in culture" over the past thirty years and that his decision to cohabitate should not reflect negatively upon his moral standards. The appellate court disagreed. It dismissed the father's argument, stating, "In concluding that the moral standards factor weighed in favor of [the mother] . . . We agree with the trial court."

The Mystifying Curative Power of Marriage

Marriage can negate intrusive and arguably unwarranted morality concerns that threaten parental custody. It can also protect parents in cases where moral fitness concerns are clearly justified. For example, in the 1990 New Mexico case *Leszinske v. Poole*, the mother entered a sexual relationship with her uncle while married to her children's father and continued the relationship after the parties' separation. The father then sought custody on the grounds that the mother's incestuous relationship could prove damaging to the children. Shockingly, the court denied the father's request. According to the court, an incestuous relationship is only concerning outside of marriage. Once the mother married the uncle, which she had to do in a foreign jurisdiction because no US state would permit the marriage, the court dismissed the change in custody petition.

An even more stunning example of the curative power of marriage is the 1998 Alabama case *K.T.W.P. v. D.R.W.* Here the mother and her new husband were literally having sex in front of the child. The couple shared a bedroom with the child and engaged in sexual relations as she slept. When learning of this sleeping arrangement, the child's father sought a change in custody. During the hearing, the court asked the stepfather if the child ever witnessed their sexual activity, and he flippantly replied, "Well, that's part of living with a man, sleeping with a woman." The mother also admitted that she and the stepfather had sexual relations with the child in the room, but justified it by stating "not while she was watching." Unmarried parents have lost custody for far less, yet the *K.T.W.P.* judge just shrugged and told the mother — and the father! — that in the future, they should both try not to have sex in front of the child.

The custodial advantages of remarriage for fathers also extend to cases where morality is not at issue. In a typical custody dispute between a mother and a father, courts will weigh the relative merits of the two parents. However, if the father is remarried, many courts will also compare the mother against the stepmother. This is especially true when the stepmother, but not the mother, is a homemaker. The 1990 Arkansas case *Puzzuoli v. Puzzuoli* is typical. In *Puzzuoli*, the court declared both parents fit, but awarded custody to the father because his new wife was a homemaker. The court found the father's home preferable, because the child would be cared for by a stepparent as opposed to the day care center his mother planned to use. By giving custody to the father, the court stated the child would now be "part of a family."

The 2001 Alaska case *West v. West* is similar. In *West*, the court held that because the father planned to get remarried, he could provide a better home environment, meaning a "two-parent household," than the unmarried mother. In explaining its decision, the court noted, "It's likely that [the father] will remarry . . . And that's a situation that, I think, is very positive because of the number of adults it provides in a household for child-rearing. It's likely that's going to happen. I think highly likely in the near future. And that there would be two adults in that household, part of the immediate family, that would be available most of the time." The *West* court then granted custody to the father.

More recent cases also demonstrate the continuing custodial benefits of remarriages. For example, in the 2017 Indiana case *Meyers v. Meyers*, the court held that the father's remarriage was a substantial factor in its decision to order a change in custody. It noted, "Father has a stable income, a stable home, and stable relationship with his new wife. This Court recognizes that this change of custody will be difficult on the children; however, this will result in the long-term emotional and psychological well-being of the children." Likewise, in the 2018 Alabama case *Sylvester v. Cartee*, the court granted the newly remarried father's change in custody petition because he had remarried, and thus, his household was now the more "stable and suitable home environment."

Social science research also confirms that fathers can gain a custodial advantage through remarriage. In their article "Effects of Divorce on Parents and Children," researchers E. Mavis Hetherington, Martha Cox, and Roger Cox examined a group of seventy-two middle-class white divorced families with a child in nursery school. All the families began the study with primary custody awarded to the mother. Over the next six years, six families experienced a change in custody, and in five of these six families, the change in custody followed the father's remarriage.

Marriage can help parents gain or keep custody of their children, but its parenthood benefits are not limited to those who already have children. Marriage also helps those seeking to become parents, particularly those struggling with infertility.

Fertility Treatment Benefits

The first documented successful fertility treatment occurred in 1785, after the famed Scottish surgeon Dr. John Hunter was approached by a man unable to impregnate his wife. The man hoped Dr. Hunter could help, and Hunter agreed to try. Hunter collected a sample of the man's sperm and inserted it into the wife's reproductive tract. Nine months later, a baby was born. Hunter had demonstrated that artificial insemination could work, but nearly a century passed before a woman was impregnated with donor sperm.

The first case of donor insemination took place in 1884, when Dr. William Pancoast of Jefferson Medical College in Philadelphia helped a childless couple conceive a baby. Pancoast invited the couple into his classroom and sedated the wife. He then obtained semen from the "best looking member of the class" and inseminated the woman while an audience of medical students sat in observation. According to his later published report, the insemination was successful and the woman subsequently gave birth to a baby boy. The mother was never told the truth of her son's conception, but the husband knew and was reputedly delighted. Years later, the son serendipitously learned

John Hunter: Founder of Scientific Surgery by Robert Thom.

of his novel beginnings when he met one of the former medical students who had witnessed his conception.

Donor-conceived children remained rare until the mid-twentieth century, when technological advances enabled the use of frozen semen. However, as artificial insemination (AI) became more common, it also became divisive. By 1945, the moral questions relating to AI were considered so pressing that when doctors and lawyers in the Chicago area planned their first Symposium on Medicolegal Problems they included AI on the agenda because "there is no subject at this time which is more controversial." The debate over AI stemmed from the use of donor sperm and the concern that such insemination was a form of adultery.

The first case to address the question of AI and adultery was a 1921 divorce decision from Canada. The case, *Orford v. Orford,* involved a married woman who became pregnant while she and her husband were living apart. Given their separation, the child could not have been Mr. Orford's, and Mrs. Orford was accused of adultery. Mrs. Orford objected to the charge by claiming her pregnancy was the result of artificial insemination. The judge didn't believe Mrs. Orford (who was probably lying) and ruled the child was the product of an extramarital affair. Nevertheless, the court noted it didn't actually matter whether Mrs. Orford was telling the truth because there was no legal difference between adultery and artificial insemination. According to the court, even if it had accepted Mrs. Orford's claim, she still would have been guilty of adultery.

American courts adopted the *Orford* reasoning and for decades afterward held that donor-conceived children were illegitimate. Finally, in 1968, this view began to change. That year, the Georgia legislature passed a statute legitimizing donor insemination for married couples, and a California court upheld the legality of AI. In both instances, the approval of AI was tied to marriage. This link was especially clear in the California court case *People v. Sorenson* in which the husband was described as a man who, "unable to accomplish his objective of creating a child by using his own semen," purchased semen from a donor "to inseminate his wife to achieve [t]his purpose." The *Sorenson* court recognized that AI did not harm marriage, rather it could help men fulfill their husbandly roles.

The reconceptualization of AI as marriage assisting, rather than threatening, helped ease the moral concerns surrounding the procedure. Soon, other courts and legislatures began adopting this view, and AI became widely accepted within the context of the marital family. Nevertheless, its use outside of marriage was treated very differently. Throughout the 1980s, many states explicitly limited AI to married couples, and even in states without an outright ban, the unmarried were still routinely denied access to this procedure. A 1985 *Harvard Law Review* article on AI noted "that only about ten percent of the doctors who perform artificial inseminations are willing to do so for unmarried women." Similarly, a 1987 survey conducted by the Office of Technology Assessment on Artificial Insemination Practice in the United States also confirmed that fertility clinics routinely refused to treat single women.

Today, approximately one-third of AI consumers in the US are unmarried women. However, accessing this technology remains much more difficult for the unmarried. Some states continue to limit AI to married couples. Others do not have specific prohibitions but permit doctors or clinics to deny treatment based on a preference for married parenthood. In the 2008 California case *North Coast Women's Care Medical Group v. Superior Court*, Guadalupe Benitez challenged a California fertility clinic's right to discriminate based on marital status, and although she prevailed on other grounds, her marital discrimination was dismissed.

Benitez and her partner were a same-sex couple who sought reproductive assistance from North Coast Medical. However, because Benitez was unmarried (same-sex marriage was not yet legal in California), her request was denied. The defendant doctors claimed that providing artificial insemination treatment to an unmarried person violated their Christian religious beliefs. The lower court ruled in favor of the clinic and held that marital status discrimination was permissible. On appeal, the California Supreme Court agreed. It held that state law did not prohibit marital status discrimination but reversed the lower court's decision because it concluded the clinic had also discriminated based on Benitez's sexual orientation. Sexual orientation discrimination was forbidden, but marital status discrimination was fine.

Shortly after the *North Coast* decision, California banned marital status discrimination. Other states have similar prohibitions. However, even these protections do not ensure that the unmarried have equal access to fertility assistance. In her article "I Got Inseminated in a Burger King Bathroom," journalist Joy Wright reveals how difficult it was for her to get artificially inseminated as an unmarried, gay woman. In the article, Wright notes that "sperm is not a scarce commodity," but that didn't mean she could "get [her] hands (or other parts) on any of it." Wright initially purchased frozen sperm from a sperm bank, but she soon ran out of money. "Do you know how expensive frozen sperm is?" she wrote. It was so expensive that Wright's friends helped her out by throwing her "a big sperm party — not a party where people brought sperm, which might have been a great idea, but a fundraiser to buy the stuff."

Given Wright's limited income and inability "to obtain sperm by the traditional no-money-down method," Wright was willing to consider extreme options, and when a stranger she met at a wellness retreat offered to provide her with sperm, she eagerly accepted. The man lived hours away from Wright, so they would meet at a Burger King halfway between their respective homes, and Wright would inseminate herself in the restaurant's bathroom. Ultimately, these insemination attempts were unsuccessful, and Wright eventually adopted. Nonetheless, her story highlights the difficulties single women continue to face when trying to access AI.

Fertility treatments are expensive, and insurance is often limited to married couples. Currently, only seventeen states mandate that private insurance plans provide some fertility coverage, and of these one-third limit it to married couples. Without a state mandate, many private insurance companies refuse to cover the unmarried. In 2022, OSF HealthCare, a private insurance company that operates 15 hospitals and 132 other facilities in Illinois and Michigan, made headlines when it narrowed its definition of *infertility* to "the inability for a married couple of the opposite sex spouses to conceive." The company readily admitted its goal was to assist only "married opposite sex spouses" to have children. OSF is a private company. However, federal and state government fertility coverage is also, often, restricted to the married. For example, the federal government covers fertility services for veterans, but only married ones. Similarly, Utah recently expanded its public employees' insurance program to cover fertility treatments — but again, only for spouses.

For those seeking fertility coverage, marriage is often the best option. In 2010, Marsha Greene quickly realized the difficulties she would face in seeking fertility treatments as an unmarried woman in Maryland. Greene and her partner were both divorced and neither wanted to remarry, but they both wanted to start a family. Unfortunately, Greene had diminished ovarian reserves and extremely low odds of conceiving naturally. Her doctors recommended fertility treatments. She was advised to begin with IUI (intrauterine insemination) and was told that if that didn't work, she should move to IVF (in vitro fertilization), which can easily run $10,000 a round. Greene had insurance, and it covered fertility treatments, but the coverage was limited to married couples. When she spoke with her insurance company, she was bluntly informed they were "unable to cover any procedure, unless it is carried out with my spouse's sperm." As long as Greene remained unmarried, she'd have to pay out of pocket. "I can afford to do this maybe three times, so I am hopeful that it will work quickly," she said. If it didn't, Greene noted she would likely get married.

Marriage and Adoption

Marriage's parenthood benefits also extend to adoption. Although no state currently requires adoptive parents to be

married, many still give married couples preference. Private
adoption officials also routinely prefer married couples over
single parents. In her article on Louisiana adoption services,
attorney Eden Bubrig recounts an interview with "Miss J," a
single woman in her forties who attempted to adopt a baby
through the Adoption Services of Catholic Charities, a non-profit
adoption agency in Louisiana. Miss J told Bubrig that she was
forcefully discouraged from attempting to adopt because she was
single. "They told me I was basically wasting my time and a lot of
my money. Because I was unmarried, I wouldn't even be considered. That was the only thing they knew about me, and at that
point, that's all they needed to know to make their decision."

Bias on the part of birth mothers can also make it harder
for the unmarried to adopt, and most are keenly aware of
this marital preference. Consequently, potential adoptive
parents may marry to increase their adoption odds. On the
online message board Wedding Wire, a woman named Kelly
explained how such considerations influenced her own marital decision. The thread began with the question, "Why get
married?" Kelly responded that in her case, it was to adopt
a child. Kelly notes that initially she and her partner were
not inclined to marry. The couple preferred a relationship that
was "more free spirited" and lacking in government involve-
ment. However, they changed their minds when they started
thinking about the adoption benefits of marriage. Kelly wrote,
"While it's not a requirement to be legally married to adopt it
greatly increases the likely hood [sic] the process will go well.
We decided we had more to gain from marriage than not,
especially long term."

Kelly was in a romantic relationship when she decided to
marry, but platonic partners also marry for parenthood benefits.
In 2009, Dear Abby received the following letter from a woman
and her friend who wished to adopt:

> Dear Abby: I consider my best friend, "Randall," to be my platonic soul mate — like a brother, only closer. Randall is gay. I am a straight female. We have no romantic interest but a deep and meaningful love nonetheless. We have talked about raising children together. In some states, there is an adoption requirement that the parents be married. Would it be considered duping friends and family to have a "real" wedding?
>
> — Platonic in Michigan

International adoptions are also easier for the married. In many foreign countries singles are barred from adopting. Many organizations that help finance international adoptions also restrict their services to the married. In her book *A History of Marriage*, Elizabeth Abbott recounts the marriage of Heather and Greg, which took place to facilitate an international adoption. The couple had lived together for fourteen years, but only married once they decided to adopt a child from China. In her wedding vows, Heather highlights their adoption plans. Standing at the altar, she tells Greg: "You're good with words. I'm good with pictures. So I won't say anything and I'll paint you a picture instead . . . I'll paint a plane flying to an unknown country to find an unknown child . . ." Heather had loved Greg for fourteen years, but she married him to adopt a baby.

Marriage's adoption benefits also extend to stepparent adoptions. When a spouse seeks to adopt their partner's child, the process is streamlined. Fitness determinations, home studies, and other procedures are usually not required. Even more important, such adoptions don't require terminating the custodial parent's rights. In contrast, when an unmarried person wishes to adopt their partner's child, the process is often difficult and sometimes impossible. In many states, an unmarried person cannot adopt their partner's child without terminating the partner's parental rights. In other states, termination is not required, but an unmarried co-parent will still need to prove parental fitness, which can mean home studies, criminal background checks, waiting periods, and multiple adoption hearings. In the case of donor-conceived children, which are common in same-sex relationships, the unmarried partner may also need affidavits from a doctor or cryobank attesting to the facts of a child's conception.

The importance of marriage for second-parent adoption was highlighted in *Obergefell v. Hodges* (the case extending the constitutional right to marriage to same-sex couples). Two of the *Obergefell* plaintiffs, April DeBoer and Jayne Rowse, were a same-sex couple living in Michigan. They were also the adoptive parents of four special-needs children. However, because Michigan law stated that only married couples or single people were permitted to adopt, the DeBoer-Rowse children only had one legal parent. DeBoer and Rowse joined the *Obergefell* litigation to secure legal rights to their children. As Rowse stated, "[We're] just two parents that want to take care of our kids and if that means going for marriage, that's what it is."

In his *Obergefell* opinion, Justice Kennedy detailed the DeBoer-Rowse story and praised the women for their efforts to achieve "the certainty and stability all mothers desire to protect their children." He then highlighted the unfairness and danger of their situation, noting that if something happened to one of the mothers, "the other would have no legal rights over the children she had not been permitted to adopt." Kennedy wrote that, because their parents could not marry, the DeBoer-Rowse children were forced to "suffer the significant material costs of being raised by unmarried parents, relegated through no fault of their own to a more difficult and uncertain family life." Ultimately, Kennedy concluded that one of the most important reasons same-sex couples must be given the right to marry was because, "without the recognition, stability, and predictability marriage offers, [same-sex couples'] children suffer the stigma of knowing their families are somehow lesser."

Reaffirming the Preference for Married Parents

Obergefell ended the custodial uncertainty faced by unmarried couples like DeBoer and Rowse, but it did so by reaffirming the long-standing notion that non-marital life, and particularly non-marital child-rearing, is inferior. As critics like law professor Katherine Franke have noted, *Obergefell* accepted the idea of "the non-married parent . . . as a site of pathology, stigma, and injury to children." Consequently, while the fight for same-sex marriage highlighted the inequality of attaching parental rights to marriage, the *Obergefell* decision ultimately helped further entrench this practice.

The rights and benefits that attach to marriage are intentionally designed to create inequality between married and unmarried parents. As law professor Elizabeth Bartholet has noted, parenthood is the only area "that our system proudly proclaims not simply the right to discriminate [on the basis of marriage] but the importance of doing so." This unfairness is then exacerbated by the fact that marriage rates are not uniform across demographics. Rich, white couples, those already at an economic and social advantage, are the group most likely to marry and thus the group most benefited by the marital parenthood preference. As law professor Dorothy Roberts notes, encouraging and protecting marital parenthood works in tandem with "the devaluation of minority childbearing." Similarly, law professor Nancy Polikoff argues that the preference for marital childbearing is particularly harmful for same-sex couples because they have few other ways to form a legal family. According to

Polikoff, recognizing only the parentage of married same-sex partners "revives the discredited distinction between 'legitimate' and 'illegitimate' children."

As long as marital and non-marital families are treated differently, marriage remains a reasonable and rational decision for those seeking to secure greater parental rights. However, not all parents can or wish to marry. By encouraging the link between marriage and parenthood, the law neglects unmarried families and exacerbates their vulnerabilities. As child welfare advocates have long argued, children are most protected when they are treated equally, without regard to their parents' marital status. Protection, not marriage, should be the ultimate goal. Currently, it is not.

chapter six

Marrying for Money Part Deux

When you marry for money, you'll earn every cent.

— AMERICAN PROVERB

When Donald Trump became president, many long-standing presidential conventions were dismissed. One of the most surprising was the delay in having his family join him in the White House. Years later, it was revealed that this delay was a bargaining tactic. Publicly, Melania claimed she was waiting because she didn't want to interrupt their son Baron's school year. Privately, she was using the delay, and the ensuing bad publicity, to successfully pressure Trump into renegotiating her prenuptial agreement.

That Melania signed a prenup is unsurprising. She was Trump's third wife, and, as everyone understood, she was marrying for money. When they met, Melania was a young, beautiful, and only moderately successful model. Trump was an aging millionaire. From the beginning, money permeated their relationship. In 2004, when Trump proposed, he "iced" the deal with a $2 million engagement ring. When Melania walked down the aisle, it was in a $100,000 pearl-and-diamond-studded wedding gown. When she said, "I do," she was given a $500,000 diamond-encrusted wedding band, and when she greeted her guests, it was in front of a $50,000 wedding cake.

During the wedding reception at Trump's Mar-a-Largo resort, a small plane crisscrossed the sky with a banner that read, MELANIA, YOU'RE HIRED. These words echoed Trump's catchphrase from his TV show *The Apprentice*. The statement also implied that

Melania Trump White House portrait.

being Trump's wife was a job and that Melania would be paid and she has been. In a *New York Post* story about Melania's marital life, it was noted that "most days, the lobby [of Trump Tower] is brimming with wardrobe boxes delivered for Melania." A different article estimated her shoe collection at more than $100,000 and her jewelry collection is worth many millions. The most stunning piece in her collection is a $3 million, twenty-five-carat diamond ring she received from Trump on their tenth wedding anniversary. It is prominently featured in her official White House portrait.

People Marry for Money

Melania Trump may be the most famous modern-day gold digger, but she is far from alone. Marrying for money is no relic of the past. In fact, the practice may be growing. As chapter 1 detailed, historically women were expected to marry for money.

IF YOU'RE A

FROG,

TURN YOURSELF

INTO A

PRINCE

Then, in the early twentieth century, acceptance of this practice largely disappeared, but the desire and the need to marry for money did not. Today, money remains a primary marriage motivation for many Americans.

In 2009, Prince & Associates, a Connecticut-based research firm focusing on the wealthy, polled a nationwide sample of 1,134 people and found that two-thirds of women and half of men would marry "an average-looking person" they liked for money. Similarly, a 2011 study by the websites ForbesWomen and YourTango found that 75 percent of women said they would not marry someone who was unemployed, and 41 percent said they wouldn't marry someone who earned significantly less than them. Most recently, a 2019 survey released by Merrill Edge, an online discount brokerage and division of Bank of America, revealed that 56 percent of Americans would choose money over love, valuing a partner who provides financial security more than one for whom they are "head over heels."

Money remains such an important relationship factor that many singles will refuse a first date if the potential partner appears to lack funds. A revealing 2016 poll conducted by the online dating service Match.com showed that owners of older smartphone models are 56 percent less likely to get a date than singles who own the latest, and most expensive, technology. Men, in particular, understand the role money plays in their dating prospects. A 2022 survey conducted by the personal credit company Credello found that a shocking 41 percent of men were willing to take on substantial debt in order to financially impress a new love interest.

"People want the money, it's not a big secret," explains Russ Alan Prince, an expert on the wealthy. In an article on marrying for money, Prince notes that people are well aware of the ways their lives could improve with additional funds and describes the calculus as something like the following: "If I had a million dollars, I don't have to do this nonsense job anymore." According to Prince, "It's not a sin to want the good life. Let's be realistic. Money doesn't buy happiness, but it solves a lot of problems." Economist Laurence Kotlikoff echoes these sentiments. In a 2022 opinion piece for CNBC, Kotlikoff writes, "We humans have the capacity to fall in love with lots of people. And there's no shame in targeting your swooning on someone who can provide you with a higher standard of living . . . Put it this way: If two people are the same in most respects, except one earns twice as much as the other, don't flip a coin. Go for the higher earner, and yes, marry for money."

Single women frequently heed this advice, and many will actually move to be closer to rich men. In her article "Sex and the City," economics professor Lena Edlund notes it is no coincidence that cities with the highest proportion of wealthy men also have some of the lowest male-to-female ratios. The national average is 97 men to 100 women, yet in Boston and New York the ratio is 94 men to 100 women, and in Philadelphia and DC, it's a paltry 90 men to 100 women. Rich men are aware of their "buying power" on the dating market. A 2016 study published in the journal *Frontiers in Psychology* showed that the more money men had, the less satisfied they were with their partner's physical appearance. However, the practice of using money to interest a spouse is not limited to the wealthy. It is present at all income levels and becomes particularly widespread when women are scarce.

A 2012 study found that reading a single article about female scarcity was enough to change male financial behavior and convince them to significantly increase the amount of money they spent on a potential marriage partner. This study also confirmed that scarcity effects were not limited to men. When the female participants read the same articles, they also expected men to raise their spending.

For some, marrying for money can be a path to riches, but for others, it is simply a way to avoid becoming poor. Single people worry about money. A 2017 study by the financial services company Northwestern Mutual found that 55 percent of single women and 49 percent of single men were unhappy with their financial situations. It also found that single people were nearly twice as likely as married people to feel financially insecure and that such worries increase with age. As Boston psychotherapist Abby Rodman told MarketWatch, "Nothing spells financial anxiety more than the threat of growing old impoverished. So, if you don't have enough money, where will you get it? Marrying someone who has some wealth is one way to sidestep that potentially bleak future."

Financial concerns are also a common reason relationships end. In his book *The Marriage-Go-Round*, sociologist Andrew Cherlin recounts a conversation with a woman who had recently terminated a long-term relationship with her insolvent partner.

"Money means . . . stability," she told Cherlin. "I don't want to struggle; if I'm in a partnership, then there's no more struggling, and income-wise we were both still struggling." This woman wasn't looking to get rich, but she did expect her relationship to make her financially stable. In this view, she is far from alone. In fact, the number of people marrying due to financial anxiety may be increasing. A 2022 Match.com report revealed that 30 percent of singles state that due to inflation, they are now looking for a financially stable partner. The same year, a survey by WalletHub found that, compared with the previous year, 37 percent more Americans said they wouldn't marry someone with bad credit.

The Fear of Marrying for Money

Mixing love and money is widespread, yet it remains taboo. In 2003, Fox tapped in to these financial anxieties with the dating show *Joe Millionaire*. The show featured a handsome construction worker and twenty beautiful women who, incorrectly, believed he was a millionaire. "Joe" dates the women and tries to figure out which have genuine feelings for him and which are only interested in his *non-existent* millions. Then, in the season finale, Joe's true financial status is revealed, and the remaining woman must decide if she's still interested. The final episode was watched by 34.6 million viewers. That year, only the Super Bowl had a larger TV audience.

American men are inundated with warnings to protect their cash, and their hearts, from unscrupulous women. Rapper Kanye West's song "Gold Digger" is typical:

> *18 years, 18 years*
> *She got one of yo' kids, got you for 18 years*

Evan Marriott, "Joe Millionaire."

I know somebody payin' child support for one of his kids
His baby momma car and crib is bigger than his is
You will see him on TV any given Sunday
Win the Super Bowl and drive off in a Hyundai.

Men's pro sports leagues like the NFL and NBA further exacerbate such fears and even run seminars to educate rookies on the dangers of gold diggers. At one of these seminars, former NFL pro Irving Fryar infamously cautioned a room of young players, "The C.I.A. has nothing on a woman with a plan." NBA star LeBron James similarly warned, "Watch your money, and watch out for women." In reflecting on these lessons, Giants lineman Jeff Hatch noted, "You'd think that women were an evil, evil species." In fact, many men do. As Canadian journalist Sabrina Maddeaux notes, "The mere mention of a gold digger is enough to prompt a litany of unsupported and borderline misogynist propaganda to spew from [men's] mouths."

In recent years, businesses have sought to capitalize on gold-digging fears by offering to protect men from potentially mercenary women. One such company is the online dating site Millionairematch.com, which was created to match wealthy singles with other wealthy singles and weed out gold diggers through income verification. Upscale dating agencies offer similar services. The famous NYC matchmaker Janis Spindel, owner of Club J-Love, charges men between $50,000 and $250,000 to pre-screen for "riff raff and gold diggers." Similarly, Samantha Daniels, founder of the elite matchmaking service Samantha's Table, states that clients pay top dollar for her "gold digger radar" and boasts she "can smell women from a mile away who only care about money."

Financial fears are one reason marrying for money is so widely condemned. A second, but equally pervasive concern, is the belief that money corrupts love. In a 2005 article, *New York Times* columnist David Brooks expressed a version of this fear when he lamented the increasing use of separate checking accounts by married couples. According to Brooks, husbands and wives were forgetting the distinction "between the individualistic ethos of the market and the communal ethos of the home." He warned then that "a union based on love can easily turn into a merger based on self-interest, where the main criterion becomes: Am I getting a good return on my investment?"

In her book *Contested Commodities*, law professor Margaret Radin writes about this fear of mixing love and money and the long-standing belief that if the commodified version of a thing exists, then the non-commodified versions will cease to exist. As the famous MasterCard ad once proclaimed, "There are some things money can't buy." Love is assumed to be one of these "things."

Men who fear gold diggers will often force a potential spouse to "prove" their love by disclaiming any financial interest in the marriage. A revealing study on the use of prenups in New York showed that these agreements are often used as a gold-digging litmus test. One attorney interviewed for the study recounted a particularly telling incident in which he was asked to draft a prenup with "egregious" terms. After receiving the document, the client insisted his fiancée sign it. She reluctantly agreed, but as soon as she acquiesced, the man capitulated and said it was no longer necessary. As the attorney explained, "Because she said she would do it, [the man knew] 'ok, you're not marrying me for my money.'" She had passed his test.

Gold-digging tests are considered necessary because marital deception is rarely actionable. The law expects that romantic partners will lie and will protect spouses when they do. The 1943 decision in *Nereni v. Nereni* is illustrative. Here a young woman sought an annulment after discovering her new husband had concealed a serious medical condition, but the court refused her request. According to the court, "No draconian law could or should be formulated to stop a man or maid from pursuing during courtship the harmless deceptive arts to which both almost universally resort by wrapping themselves in an aura which is not strictly theirs to use." The court claimed everyone lies when they're courting and held there is nothing wrong with tricking a potential spouse with "a bewitching glass eye or a set of pearly false teeth." Such lies, said the court, are to be expected. Concealing one's financial motives also does not render a marriage invalid.

In her book *Intimate Lies*, law professor Jill Hasday notes that lying about money is common among romantic partners, yet "courts are reluctant to award remedies when financial deception occurs within marriage." This is true even when the financial motives are blatant. In the 2013 case *In re Estate of Smallman*, the Tennessee court acknowledged that a woman who married her husband two weeks before he died was a "bad person" and "gold digger," but held these facts were still not a proper basis for invalidating a marriage. *Smallman* is not unique. In fact, courts rarely sympathize with a tricked partner. For example, in the stunning 1975 New York case *Avnery v. Avnery*, the gold-digging husband repeatedly lied about his affection for the moneyed wife, yet the court admonished the woman. In denying the wife's annulment claim, the court condescendingly noted, "The fraud required for an annulment must be 'of such a nature as to deceive an ordinary prudent person' not an ordinary woman in love." More recently, in the 2010 case *Flowers v. Flowers*, the court accepted the husband's claim that the wife was a gold digger who held no romantic feelings for him but found her financial motives irrelevant. It callously declared, "Later-in-life marriages are often entered into for reasons other than a sexual relationship."

Benefits of Marrying for Money

The widespread fear of gold digging obscures the fact that most marriages are, at least in part, economic arrangements. Legally, marriage is an agreement to pool resources, financial and otherwise, for the benefit of the couple. It is also an assur-

Shaniqua Tompkins.

ance that, should the marriage end, both spouses are entitled to a share of these jointly accumulated assets. These are important protections, yet they are almost impossible to secure outside of marriage. Despite the rising rates of non-marital cohabitation, most states refuse to recognize the shared property interests of unmarried intimates. Marriage is the only way most romantic partners can receive a portion of the property they helped accumulate. Shaniqua Tompkins, the longtime girlfriend of rapper Curtis Jackson, a.k.a. 50 Cent, learned this lesson the hard way.

Tompkins and Jackson were in a romantic relationship for twelve years, but never married. Then, when the relationship ended, Tompkins sought financial compensation from Jackson. According to Tompkins, she and Jackson agreed that she would provide the domestic and homemaking services, including the care of the couple's child, that allowed Jackson to devote himself to his music. In return, Tompkins would share in Jackson's future financial success. If the couple had married, such an agreement would have been unnecessary. Spouses have a legal right to a share of all property accumulated during the relationship. In addition, a spouse's homemaking services may also entitle them to alimony. However, because Tompkins was only a girlfriend, the court held that the work she provided, taking care of the home and the child (the same services she would be compensated for as a wife), was "of a nature which would ordinarily be exchanged without expectation of pay." The court rejected her economic claim and dismissed her case as nothing more than an "unfortunate tale of a love relationship gone sour."

If women want to be compensated for their relationship efforts, they must marry, and they are expected to know this. In the 1994 Mississippi case *Davis v. Davis*, the court stated this rule explicitly. *Davis* involved an unmarried couple, Elvis and Travis Davis, who had lived together for thirteen years. On at least one occasion, and possibly several, Travis asked Elvis to marry him. Elvis declined, but her refusal did not end the relationship. For more than a decade, Elvis devoted herself to caring for Travis and their family. Elvis testified that she took care of the home and the children (both her child with Travis, as well as his children from a previous relationship) and did innumerable other household tasks including cooking, gardening, sewing, and painting. Due to these efforts, Travis was able to devote himself to his businesses — which grew significantly during the couple's relationship. When they met, Travis had a net worth of $850k. When the relationship ended, he had more than $7 million in assets. Elvis argued that she had a right to a share of this increase, but the Mississippi Supreme Court disagreed. According to the court, if Elvis had wanted compensation for her domestic services, she should have married. "When opportunity knocks, one must answer its call," wrote the court. Because Elvis "failed to do so," the court held, "her claim is all for naught."

Theoretically, unmarried partners have the same right of contract as all other non-married parties, but in practice, they do not. Cohabitants are held to a higher standard of formality. As law professor Courtney Joslin writes, "The law authorizes courts to recognize joint business partnerships or ventures that exist in fact, even in the absence of formalities, express agreements, or even an understanding of the consequences of the parties' conduct. But courts refuse to apply these principles equally to recognize and give effect to the joint endeavor of starting and running a family. Instead, for this venture alone, formalities are required." When romantic partners seek compensation for "housewifely services," tasks such as cooking, cleaning, laundry, caring for children, paying bills, or the countless other things that keep a household running, their requests are rarely granted. Legally, the dividing line for compensation is marriage. Whether this distinction is equitable is a different question.

A 2009 study by Professors Stanford Braver and Ira Mark Ellman suggests that most people find marriage-based distinctions far from fair. The study asked a random sample of adults to examine a series of heterosexual relationship vignettes and determine whether the man should pay the woman alimony after the relationship ended. Respondents, regardless of income, marital status, gender, or political affiliation, did not view marriage as the key factor in determining whether a romantic partner should be entitled to financial support. Instead, most awarded alimony based on perceived need and were willing to award support to an unmarried partner, even when such awards would not be permissible under the law. Braver and Ellman describe this rejection of the marriage-based distinction as "telling" and suggest "it is American law, not our respondents, that is peculiar."

Marriage protects the non-moneyed party's economic interests in the relationship. However, both spouses can benefit when economic motivations are clear. As sociologist Viviana A. Zelizer explains, "Economic activity and intimacy intersect all the time, and frequently create 'good matches.'" According to Zelizer, a "good match" doesn't mean that "you and I would approve of the bargain or that the match is equal and just. Instead, [it] mean[s] that the match is viable: It gets the economic work of the relationship done and sustains the relationship." Consider the following ad placed in a 1985 issue of the *San Francisco Chronicle*. It reads:

> Attractive & successful young businessman, 32, would like to meet only a beautiful & classy lady 18-39 who is tired of working hard & wants to live well. I am only interested in a permanent living together relationship / marriage without children. Prefer someone with experience. Or interest in Real Estate to help me with my business.

The ad's author was offering money in exchange for a wife with looks, class, and "experience." This was not altruism; he clearly expected to benefit from this exchange. More recent examples of such offers can be found on the dating website MillionaireMatch .com. The site was initially founded to connect wealthy singles to other wealthy singles (and explicitly exclude gold diggers), but many of the site's rich male clients were more interested in finding women with good looks rather than high incomes. Consequently, the site now includes many beautiful, non-moneyed women who are specifically looking for rich men. As one review notes, "These women are attractive enough to be extremely picky about only dating real millionaires. The 'Certified Millionaire' diamond on your profile will draw them in like moths to a flame."

Although it is rarely acknowledged, marrying for money is often the only realistic opportunity most women have for

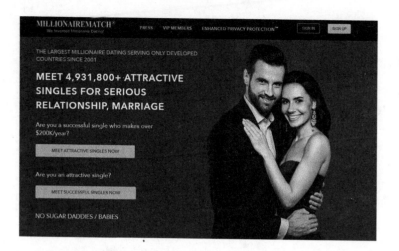

acquiring significant wealth. The average American woman earns only 84 percent of what men earn, and this gender wage gap has remained stagnant for decades. For the ultra-wealthy, this wealth difference is even more extreme. In 2022, only 13 percent of the world's billionaires were women. The percentage of female multimillionaires is nearly identical. In the United States, only 13.5 percent of millionaires are female, and the percentage who earned their wealth is even lower. Not a single one of the top ten richest women on *Forbes*'s 2022 list earned her fortune. Forty percent received their wealth from their husbands while the remaining 60 percent inherited it from other family members. As journalist Sabrina Maddeaux notes, "All the leaning in and hard work in the world won't change the fact that, even today, a self-made wealthy woman is a statistical unicorn." Thus, Maddeaux praises women who marry for money, describing them as the "front liners in the fight for class, economic and gender equality"

Marrying for money also benefits women at the other end of the financial spectrum and may be preferable to the other financial arrangements women use to make ends meet. In 2015, more than a quarter million American women signed up to

become "sugar babies" on the website SeekingArrangement
.com. The site connects young women with "sugar daddies"
who, in exchange for dates and other relationship perks, finance
their lifestyle. Some "sugar babies" are looking for fancy vaca-
tions or luxury goods, but many are primarily interested in
tuition payments. It is no coincidence that more than a third
of the eight million women on these sites are students. In fact,
SeekingArrangement.com explicitly targets college students and
gives free upgrades to those who register with an .edu address.
The site boasts, "When their biological dads can't pay for college,
Sugar Daddies are stepping up."

Websites like SeekingArrangement tap in to the real financial
anxiety that many young women face after graduation. Studies
show that women take significantly longer to pay off their
student debts than men and that a whopping 53 percent of female
debtors (compared with 39 percent of men) are paying more in
student loan payments than they can reasonably afford. This
debt can then make it harder for women to change careers, start
their own businesses, or take lower-paying "dream" jobs. It can
also make it hard to simply survive. According to the American
Association of University Women, "Student debt is making it
nearly impossible for many women to afford their basic living

expenses after graduating from college." Add children into the mix and the effects are even starker. The average single mother does not have enough funds to cover the costs of childcare. This financial insufficiency then makes further debt more likely and saving for things like retirement nearly impossible.

Given the financial uncertainty facing many "sugar babies," it is not surprising that many will marry their "daddies" if given the opportunity. Brandon Wade, founder and CEO of SeekingArrangement.com, encourages such unions. "Women have married for economic reasons since the beginning of time. If you find a sugar daddy that is looking to settle down, then you're guaranteed a husband that will spoil and take care of you." Notably, Wade is not alone in promoting marriage as a solution to female financial distress. As discussed in chapter 2, federal, state, and local governments have long encouraged poor women to marry for money. In 1992, Vice President Dan Quayle gave a speech declaring marriage "the best anti-poverty program there is." Since then, countless politicians have echoed these sentiments and backed them up with monetary incentives. In the 1990s, states like Wisconsin and New Jersey enacted bride-fare programs that provided recipients with increased monthly benefit payments, as well as the ability to exclude more income from the benefits eligibility calculation, if they agreed to marry. Then, in 1996, Congress passed the Personal Responsibility and Work Opportunity Act, which made marriage the centerpiece of welfare reforms.

Opponents of government marital initiatives have tended to focus on the perceived harms of marital commodification. Hannah Rosenthal, executive director of the Wisconsin Women's Council, a research and advocacy group, called bride-fare programs "dressed-up marriage brokering for poor people." She noted, "It's dangling a paycheck in front of a girl and saying, 'We'll give you a bonus if you get married.'" Sociologist Walter

Williams voiced similar concerns. "Marriage is much deeper than some government program," he said. "When you stand in front of the minister, you're supposed to be there because you love the person and are committed to them, not because you're going to get $80. That's a tainted marriage from the beginning. That trivializes marriage. If $80 will do it, that is bad news." Critics like Williams and Rosenthal condemn the commodification of marriage and assume love matches are preferable. That is debatable. Sometimes, the better marital option is getting paid.

Jacqueline Kennedy, whose first marriage was famously plagued by infidelities, once stated, "The first time you marry for love, the second for money . . ." Similarly, in the legendary gold-digger movie *How to Marry a Millionaire*, Schatze Page (played by Lauren Bacall) decides to marry for money only after her first marriage, a love match, leads to financial ruin. Early in the movie, Schatze informs her housemates she is divorced and Loco (Betty Grable) responds, "Oh then you must be loaded." Schatze replies:

> No. Mine was one of those divorces you *don't* read about. The wife finished second . . . I was absolutely nuts about that guy. You know what he did to me? First off, he gives me a phony name. Second, it turns out he was already married! Third, from the minute the preacher said amen, he never did another tap of work. The next thing I knew he'd stolen my television set and given it to a car hop. And when I asked him how about that, he hits me with a chicken!

As Schatze learned, love doesn't prevent financial exploitation; sometimes it facilitates it.

The prenup "test" described earlier in this chapter highlights love's potential for financial abuse. Such tests are ostensibly used

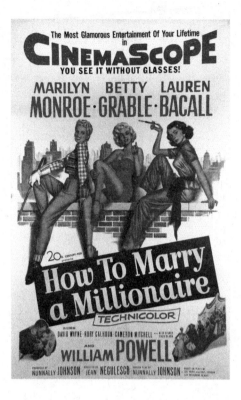

to ensure the non-moneyed party is marrying for love, but the moneyed party's intention to deny their future spouse a share of the marital property typically receives little scrutiny. The purpose of a prenup is to alter the default marital property rules and prevent the sharing of marital money upon divorce. When the less wealthy party is forced to "prove" their love with a prenup, they are also being forced to give up their financial rights. This financial manipulation is then exacerbated by the fact that parties are typically unrealistic about the prospect of divorce and thus the likelihood of their prenup ever coming into effect.

When women assert their value and negotiate for it, they protect themselves from potential financial exploitation, yet the successful gold digger is rarely praised. In her best-selling book *Primates of Park Avenue*, author Wednesday Martin writes about the "trophy wives" of Manhattan's Upper East Side. The book is full of juicy tidbits about the extravagant lives of these ultra-rich women and includes the revelation that many receive end-of-year "wife bonuses." Martin writes:

> A wife bonus, I was told, might be hammered out in a pre-nup or post-nup, and distributed on the basis of not only how well her husband's fund had done but her own performance — how well she managed the home budget, whether the kids got into a "good" school — the same way their husbands were rewarded at investment banks. In turn these bonuses were a ticket to a modicum of financial independence and participation in a social sphere where you don't just go to lunch, you buy a $10,000 table at the benefit luncheon a friend is hosting.

More than any other revelation in the book, Martin's discussion of "wife bonuses" caused an uproar. In one review, *Chicago Tribune* writer Gina Barecca condescendingly described these payments as the reward women received "from their conspicuously powerful husbands for staying lithe, keeping the domestic staff in good order and rearing high-achieving children — think *Pretty Woman*, except Julia Roberts has a law degree she doesn't use." Barecca then quotes a friend who described these marriages as "tennis relationships," because "love means nothing." Caitlin Moscatello, of *Glamour* magazine, was similarly appalled by Martin's "wife bonuses" but voiced different criticisms. She described such payments as "demeaning" and wrote, "At its worst, the payment structure magnifies patriarchal marriage to the point where it hurts the eyes . . . He's her husband, yes, but he also becomes *her boss*. She reports to him, spends her days trying to impress him, and he evaluates her. And as his earning potential presumably grows with the progression of his career, she in turn becomes increasingly dependent on him over time."

What these criticisms fail to acknowledge is that the alternative to "demeaning" bonuses is simply not getting paid. It is commonly estimated that services provided by the average stay-at-home mom are worth almost $200,000 per year. Nevertheless, no court will force a husband to make such payments. The law literally declares such services priceless, meaning they can't be paid for. Tellingly, anti-commodification arguments usually arise when it's women who wish to receive money for something not, as law professor Katharine Silbaugh notes, "when things typically associated with male personhood are being sold." The California case of *Borelli v. Bruseau* exemplifies such treatment.

In *Borelli*, the husband suffered a debilitating stroke and subsequently required full-time care. He asked his wife to provide this care but also recognized this would be an extraordinary physical and emotional burden. Therefore, the husband promised to amend his will to compensate his wife for these services and, relying on this promise, the wife agreed to become her husband's full-time caregiver. Unfortunately, the husband did not keep his end of the bargain. Instead of amending his will to reflect his wife's sacrifices, he left nearly all his property to a daughter from a previous marriage. When the wife discovered the husband had reneged on their deal, she sued his estate to recover the property she had been promised. She lost. According to the *Borelli* court, spouses have a duty of care to each other, and the wife did nothing more than what a good and loving wife was already obligated to do. The court wrote, "Even if few things are left that cannot command a price, marital support remains one of them."

The idea that domestic services should be provided gratuitously is a remnant of the deeply gendered doctrine of coverture. Coverture meant that a wife's labor was owned by her husband, and thus he had no obligation to pay for the domestic services she provided. Married women are no longer bound by the law of coverture, yet wives still cannot be paid for their contributions to a marriage. The only thing that has changed is the justification. Now courts claim caretaking services can't be compensated not because the husband owns this labor, but because such compensation taints love and harms the institution of marriage.

When women marry for money, they reject the idea that domestic work should be provided for free. They also challenge the idea that marrying for love is always best. The modern love match is based on a very specific idea of love — one that is increasingly recognized as problematic. Sociologist Andrew Cherlin calls modern love "a very selfish form of love." He characterizes it as, "Marry as long as it is personally fulfilling and leave when it gets hard or less fun even if children are hurt." Tellingly, Cherlin is not alone in holding this cynical view of contemporary marriage. In their article "The Suffocation of Marriage," Professors Finkel, Hui, Carsweel, and Larson argue that modern spouses are asking too much of marriage and suggest that the "emphasis on higher needs — has undermined spouses' marital quality and personal well-being." To illustrate their point, they cite the famous singleton Carrie Bradshaw, from the show *Sex and the City*. In the episode "American Girl in Paris Part Deux," Bradshaw proclaims, "Well maybe it is time to be clear about who I am. I am someone who is looking for love. Real love. Ridiculous, inconvenient, consuming, can't-live-without-each-other love." According to Finkel and his colleagues, those who desire this type of demanding and ultimately unattainable love are headed for disappointment. As an alternative, they suggest a marriage based on more tangible needs, needs that are more easily met. Marrying for money is one example.

The Problem with Marrying for Money

Forty years before Shaniqua Tompkins sued 50 Cent, Michelle Triola sought compensation from her former boyfriend, actor Lee Marvin. At Marvin's insistence, Triola gave up her own acting career and devoted herself full-time to caring for his needs. Then, when the relationship ended, she sought reimbursement for her sacrifices. The resulting *Marvin* litigation is famous because it is one of the few instances when a court granted compensation to an unmarried cohabitant. Nevertheless, rather than usher in a new appreciation of women's caretaking services, the decision had the opposite effect.

In 1979, *Saturday Night Live* parodied the Triola lawsuit. Original cast members Jane Curtin and Dan Aykroyd squared off in a "Point–Counterpoint" exchange satirizing Triola's request. The segment began with Curtin taking the pro-Triola position: "A woman in this modern-day relationship may well

Michelle Triola and Lee Marvin.

give up all her own personal pursuits . . . to give her full support
to her man's career. Michelle is just asking that the courts recognize that reality . . . There is an old saying, behind every successful man there's a woman, a loving, giving, caring woman."

Aykroyd responds, "Jane, you ignorant slut," and proceeds
to equate Triola with a prostitute. "Bagged out, dried up, slunk
meat like you and Michelle Triola know the rules, if you want
a contract sign on the dotted line . . . I guess what you and
Michelle are saying is that when you're on your backs, the meter
is running."

Aykroyd ridiculed the idea of compensating women for their
domestic labor. He was playing a boorish character in a satirical
sketch and yet, the view he expressed is the one that endures.
When women seek to enforce economic agreements made
within the context of a relationship, they are treated as undeserving and contemptible. The Anna Nicole Smith inheritance
battle is one of the most famous examples.

Smith was accustomed to being paid for her beauty. She
began her career as an exotic dancer and model and in 1993,
became *Playboy* magazine's Playmate of the Year. The following year, at age twenty-six, Smith married the eighty-nine-year-
old billionaire oil tycoon J. Howard Marshall. Marshall was a
cunning and sophisticated business player who understood that
if he wished to enjoy Smith's youth and exceptional beauty, he
would need to compensate her accordingly. Marshall promised
to provide for Smith and she agreed to marry him, but when
he died thirteen months later, Smith was left almost nothing.
When Smith challenged her financial exclusion, she was labeled
a "gold digging monster." The duplicitous Marshall was remem-
bered as a naive, lovesick fool.

Those who supported Smith's claim viewed the marriage as
a reciprocal relationship that greatly benefited Marshall. As
journalist Carol Sarler noted, the Smith-Marshall marriage

was a "deal freely entered into by adults who understood each other. Perfectly." Journalist Sarah Marshall also described it as a mutually beneficial exchange and suggested the backlash against Smith was because she was a woman who knew her own worth. Marshall wrote, "The only person more deserving of [public] humiliation than the cluelessly beautiful woman is the beautiful woman who, even more unforgivably, *knows* she is beautiful: the woman who knows she is worth something to the world, and leverages her value to escape a life she can no longer stand. The woman who looks back at a world that always wants something from her, and asks, *How bad do you want it? How much are you willing to pay?*"

In 2007, the following post appeared on an online message board from a woman seeking a rich husband:

> What am I doing wrong? Okay I am tired of beating around the bush. I am a beautiful (spectacularly beautiful) 25-year-old girl. I am articulate and classy. I'm not from New York. I'm looking to get married to a guy who makes at least half a million a year. I know how [*sic*] that sounds like a lot, but keep in mind that a million a year is middle class in New York City, so I don't think I'm overreaching at all. Are there guys who make $500k or more on this board? Any wives? Could you send me tips? I dated a businessman who makes average around $200–250. But that's where I seem to hit a roadblock. $250,000 won't get me to central park west. I know a woman in my yoga class who was married to an investment banker and lives in Tribeca, and she's not as pretty as I am, nor is she a great genius. So what is she doing right? How do I get to her level? . . . How do you decide marriage vs. just girlfriend? I am looking for

MARRIAGE ONLY. Please hold your insults —
I'm putting myself out there in an honest way. Most
beautiful women are superficial; at least I'm being up
front about it. I wouldn't be searching for these kinds
of guys if I wasn't about to match them — in looks,
culture, sophistication, and keeping a nice home and
hearth.

The poster received the following answer:

I read your posting with great interest and have
thought meaningfully about your dilemma. I offer
the following analysis of your predicament. Firstly,
I'm not wasting your time, I qualify as a guy who
fits your bill; that is I make more than $500K per
year. That said here's how I see it. Your offer from the
prospective [*sic*] of a guy like me, is plain and simple a
crappy business deal. Here's why. Cutting through all
the B.S., what you suggest is a simple trade: you bring
your looks to the party and I bring my money. Fine,
simple. But here's the rub, your looks will fade and
my money will likely continue into perpetuity . . . in
fact, it is very likely that my income increases but it
is an absolute certainty that you won't be getting any
more beautiful!

So in economic terms you are a depreciating asset
and I am an earning asset. Not only are you a depreciating asset, your depreciation accelerates! Let me
explain, you're 25 now and will likely stay pretty hot
for the next 5 years, but less so each year. Then the
fade begins in earnest. By 35 stick a fork in you! So
in Wall Street terms, we would call you a trading
position, not a buy and hold . . . hence the rub . . .

marriage. It doesn't make good business sense to "buy you" (which is what you're asking) so I'd rather lease. In case you think I'm being cruel, I would say the following. If my money were to go away so would you, so when your beauty fades I need an out. It's as simple as that. So a deal that makes sense is dating not marriage . . . By the way, you could always find a way to make your own money and then we wouldn't need to have this difficult conversation. With all that said, I must say you're going about it the right way. Classic "pump and dump."

I hope this is helpful, and if you want to enter into some sort of lease, let me know.

The above exchange may have been fabricated, but the issues it raises are genuine. As the responder points out, the two are only having this conversation because the poster hasn't found a way to make $500,000 per year herself. The responder implies that marrying for money is the lazy path to riches and suggests if the poster had just tried harder, she could have become rich through her own career accomplishments. This assumption is the problem.

When women marry for money, it is typically because they can't earn it themselves. For years, studies on mating preferences have demonstrated that men tend to focus on physical attractiveness while women are more interested in men's resource acquisition. One explanation for these results has been that they reveal innate evolutionary differences. Male choice reflects women's time-limited reproductive capabilities, while female choice represents a desire to find men who have the resources to help raise their children. More recent studies challenge this idea and show that when women's economic opportunities increase, their interest in marrying for money diminishes.

In their paper "Stepping Out of the Caveman's Shadow: Nations' Gender Gap Predicts Degree of Sex Differentiation in Mate Preferences," UK researchers Marcel Zentner and Klaudia Mitura show that the supposed evolutionary biases in mate choice decline proportionally with nations' gender parity. In their study, 3,177 respondents completed an online mate preference survey. The respondents came from ten countries, ranging from Finland, where there was low gender disparity, to Turkey, where the gender gap was extremely high. They were then asked whether certain criteria — such as financial prospects and being a good cook — were important considerations when choosing a mate. They found that gender difference in mate preferences were "highest in gender-unequal societies, and smallest in the most gender-equal societies." Such research suggests that as societies become more gender-equal, men and women increasingly seek the same qualities in a partner. Women also like attractive partners, but they will forgo sex appeal to achieve financial security. The Smith-Marshall marriage follows this pattern.

Anna Nicole Smith did not marry J. Howard Marshall for his looks. She married him because her financial future was bleak, and he offered her a way out. In describing their relationship, Smith stated, "He took me out of a terrible place, took care of me. He was my savior. It wasn't a sexual 'baby, oh baby, I love your body' type love — it was a deep thank-you for taking me out of this hole." Marriage drastically improved Smith's economic circumstances, but these improvements were temporary. As Smith discovered, marrying for money is a precarious solution to women's economic inequality and particularly to female poverty.

When the government tells low-income women to rely on men for support, it is abdicating its responsibility for solving the problems that contribute to female poverty in the first place. These problems are no secret. For the past fifty years, the inflation-adjusted hourly wage for the bottom 10 percent of female earners has remained stagnant. Worse, such low-wage jobs tend to involve fluctuating, insufficient hours and frequent layoffs. Other glaring contributors to female poverty include workplace gender discrimination, lack of safe and affordable childcare, and the devaluing of women's caretaking labor. The government could promote policies to address these problems. Instead, as law professor Lucie White notes, the government has found it easier "to point a finger at poor women and accost them to escape poverty by catching a man." Law professor Martha Fineman echoes such criticisms. In fact, she has urged the abolition of marriage as a legal category entirely, "precisely because it precludes consideration of other solutions to social problems."

When marriage is the government's answer to female poverty, the sexism in the solution is undeniable. Encouraging poor women to marry for money is also problematic because it doesn't work. Marriage can only provide women with financial stability if they marry good men with good economic prospects. One study on the effect of the government's pro-marriage welfare reforms found they didn't make poor women more likely to marry, but they did make them more likely to marry financially insolvent men. Other research showed that when poor women were forced to rely on men for support, they often wound up entering into relationships with men they had no interest in marrying.

In 1997, the state of Wisconsin unintentionally demonstrated that poor women were turning to men as a financial last resort. That year, the state selected a random group of welfare recipients to receive the full extent of their child support payments with no corresponding reduction in their welfare benefits. These increased funds were not expected to change the women's living arrangements, but they did — drastically. By 2004, women who received the extra money were significantly less likely to have cohabitated with men other than the fathers of their children. The experiment revealed that low-income women had been reluctantly relying on men for financial assistance and that when they finally had enough income to support themselves independently, they avoided these problematic, and possibly abusive, relationships.

One of the greatest problems with financial dependency is it creates the perfect conditions for domestic violence. Without sufficient assets of their own, victims of domestic abuse are often unable to leave an abuser while still providing for themselves or their children. When it is a choice between caring for their children or freeing themselves from abuse, many victims will stay with or return to an abuser. Fifteen to thirty percent of welfare recipients are victims of domestic violence, and many enter the welfare system specifically to escape from abusive relationships. Reducing government support and encouraging women to rely on men perpetuates this cycle of abuse.

Two decades into the twenty-first century, women still earn significantly less than men, their caretaking services are treated as gratuitous, and they are expected to use men as their social safety net. Given these circumstances, marrying for money is a reasonable choice, but it is also an unfair one. Oscar Wilde once said, "Who being in love is poor?" But love doesn't pay the bills. Only when women have the same economic opportunities as men will they have an equal chance to marry for love. Of course, whether they will marry without the economic incentive is a different question. Wilde also wrote, "One should always be in love. That is the reason one should never marry."

Conclusion

Mae West famously quipped, "Marriage is a fine institution, but I'm not ready for an institution." Many Americans agree, and this is considered a problem. Although much has changed over the past two centuries, the unmarried continue to inspire alarm. In the 2023 book *The Two-Parent Privilege: How Americans Stopped Getting Married and Started Falling Behind*, economist Melissa Kearney blames the unmarried for a host of societal problems and then argues that the very future of our country depends on increasing marriage. Other marriage advocates go even further. In 2022, the Institute of Family Studies released their report *Marriage Still Matters* (examining declining fertility rates across the globe) and suggested marriage may be the key to the continuation of the entire human race.

Recently, Steven Crowder, a political commentator who prides himself on his "provocative" views, extolled the importance of marriage and publicly bemoaned the fact that his wife was "allowed" to divorce him without his consent. He wrote:

> I have been living through what has increasingly been
> a horrendous divorce. Let me say from the outset, to
> be clear, there was no infidelity or any kind of phys-
> ical abuse on either side. And no, this was not my
> choice. My then-wife decided she didn't want to be
> married anymore. And in the State of Texas, that is
> completely permitted. It's been the most heartbreak-
> ing experience of my life, what I consider to be my
> deepest personal failure . . . Children need a mom
> and a dad, and divorce is horrible. But in today's legal

system, my beliefs don't matter. In Texas, divorce is permitted when one party wants it, period.

Crowder's criticisms echo growing Republican proposals to bolster marriage by limiting the grounds for divorce. During the 2016 Republican National Convention, delegates considered adding language to their party's platform declaring, "Children are made to be loved by both natural parents united in marriage. Legal structures such as No-Fault Divorce, which divides families and empowers the state, should be replaced by a Fault-based Divorce." In the end, this proposal was not adopted, but similar language has been incorporated into state Republican party platforms.

In 2022, the Republican party of Texas added language to its platform calling for an end to no-fault divorce: "We urge the Legislature to rescind unilateral no-fault divorce laws, to support covenant marriage, and to pass legislation extending the period of time in which a divorce may occur to six months after the date of filing for divorce." In 2023, the Nebraska GOP party platform adopted similar language seeking to limit no-fault divorce "to situations in which the couple has no children." That same year, the Louisiana Republican party strongly considered endorsing a bill to eliminate the state's no-fault divorce provisions because such "laws have destroyed the institute of marriage."

If marriage were the best solution to America's economic and social problems, such marriage promotion tactics might be justified, but history has repeatedly shown it is not. At best, marriage is a Band-Aid that Americans have used when society is too sexist, too racist, or just too lazy to implement better solutions. This use of marriage has sometimes (sort of) worked, at least in the short term, but ultimately, it has been more likely to exacerbate the problems it was intended to solve. Given this dubious success record, we should be looking for different fixes to America's problems, not doubling down on marriage.

Although marriage advocates are correct when they argue that marriage remains highly beneficial, this is only because America has made the deliberate choice to benefit the married. We could make a different choice, and eventually we may. Until then, we should stop acting shocked when marital incentives work. There is no such thing as marrying for the wrong reason. When people marry for benefits, they are doing exactly what American law and policy encourages them to do — they are getting married.

1. Before reading *You'll Do*, how would you have described the purpose of marriage? Have your views changed?

2. Historically, marriage was the primary relationship around which the family was organized. What are the benefits or detriments of organizing families around the marital relationship rather than other caregiving relationships? What might a world without marriage look like?

3. Marrying for money is often seen as devaluing marriage. Do you agree? Why do Americans largely view marriage and money as incompatible?

4. Historically, married people occupied a much higher social status than the unmarried. Is this still true today? If so, is it for the same or different reasons than in the past?

5. Should marriage ever be a defense to criminal prosecution?

6. In the past, non-marital childbearing was viewed as hugely problematic. Why was this? How has this view changed, or not changed, over time?

7. What are some of the unique parenthood challenges faced by same-sex couples? Has the right to marry effectively addressed these problems?

8. Why might the traditional marital bargain remain appealing to modern couples?

9. Why are women still more likely to marry for money and men more likely to marry for attractiveness? Is this difference innate or the result of social and economic factors?

10. How much does the ability to divorce affect one's willingness to marry? What are the pros and cons of making divorce harder? What do you think would happen to marriage if it became harder to leave unhappy marriages?

11. Women tend to be the primary readers of this book. Why do you think that is? Why might women be more interested in marriage and its implications than men?